THE CHURCHES AND THE CANADIAN EXPERIENCE

THE CHURCHES
AND THE CANADIAN
EXPERIENCE

A Faith and Order Study of
The Christian Tradition

Edited by John Webster Grant
with a Foreword by David W. Hay

THE RYERSON PRESS TORONTO

Reprinted, 1966

The publication of this book at a popular price has been made possible by generous gifts from the McGill University Research Committee, the Canadian Council of Churches, the Ecumenical Affairs Committee of the Anglican Church of Canada, the Baptist Convention of Ontario and Quebec, and University of St. Michael's College, as well as by the Fund for Theological Research of The Ryerson Press.

PRINTED AND BOUND IN CANADA BY THE RYERSON PRESS

CONTENTS

CONTRIBUTORS   vii

FOREWORD *David W. Hay*   ix

EDITOR'S PREFACE *John Webster Grant*   xi

1 TRADITIONS OF THE CATHOLIC CHURCH IN FRENCH CANADA
Marcel de Grandpré   1

2 TRADITION IN THE ANGLICAN CHURCH OF CANADA *T. R. Millman*   14

3 THE CONGREGATIONAL TRADITION IN CANADA *Earl B. Eddy*   25

4 THE PRESBYTERIAN TRADITION IN CANADA *N. G. Smith*   38

5 IS THERE A CANADIAN BAPTIST TRADITION? *Stuart Ivison*   53

6 THE PEOPLE CALLED METHODISTS IN CANADA *Goldwin French*   69

7 CHANGING CHARACTERISTICS OF THE CATHOLIC CHURCH *J. A. Raftis*   82

8 LUTHERAN TRADITION IN CANADA *Walter Freitag*   94

9 CANADIAN ORTHODOXY AND THE UNION OF CHURCHES *Milos Mladenovic*   102

10 SECTARIAN TRADITION IN CANADA *John S. Moir*   119

11 BLENDING TRADITIONS: THE UNITED CHURCH OF CANADA
John Webster Grant   133

12 A CANADIAN CHRISTIAN TRADITION *H. H. Walsh*   145

CONTRIBUTORS

The Reverend DAVID W. HAY, M.A., D.D. Professor of Systematic Theology, Knox College, Toronto.

The Reverend JOHN WEBSTER GRANT, M.A., D.D., D.PHIL. Editor of The Ryerson Press. Author of *Free Churchmanship in England* (1955), *God's People in India* (1959), *The Ship under the Cross* (1960) and *George Pidgeon* (1962).

The Reverend MARCEL DE GRANDPRÉ, C.S.V., L.TH., L.PS., B.ED. Director of Research at Fédération des Collèges Classiques, Montreal. Author of *L'Éducateur et la Formation Religieuse des Adoloscents* (1958).

The Reverend T. R. MILLMAN, M.A., D.D., PH.D. Professor of Church History, Wycliffe College, Toronto. Author of *Jacob Mountain, First Lord Bishop of Quebec* (1947) and *The Life of the Right Reverend, the Honourable Charles James Stewart, Second Anglican Bishop of Quebec* (1953).

The Reverend EARL B. EDDY, B.A., B.D., TH.D. Minister of St. Luke's United Church, Hespeler, Ontario. Author of a thesis on "The Beginnings of Congregationalism in the Early Canadas."

The Reverend N. G. SMITH, M.A., D.D. Librarian and Dean of Residence, Presbyterian College, Montreal.

The Reverend STUART IVISON, B.A., B.TH. Minister, First Baptist Church, Ottawa. Joint author of *The Baptists in Upper and Lower Canada before 1820*.

GOLDWIN FRENCH, M.A. Associate Professor of History, McMaster University, Hamilton. Author of *Parsons and Politics* (1962).

The Reverend J. A. RAFTIS, C.S.B., M.A., D.ÈS SC.SOC., PH.D. Professor in the Pontifical Institute of Mediaeval Studies and the Graduate Division, Faculty of Theology, University of St. Michael's College, Toronto.

The Reverend WALTER FREITAG, B.A., B.D., S.T.M. President, The Lutheran College and Seminary, Saskatoon.

MILOS MLADENOVIC, Docteur en Droit (Paris). Formerly Professor at the University of Belgrade. Associate Professor of History, McGill University, Montreal. Author of *L'Etu Serbe en Moyen-Age* (1931).

JOHN S. MOIR, M.A., PH.D. Assistant Professor of History, Carleton University, Ottawa. Author of *Church and State in Canada West* (1959). Editor of *Ontario History*, 1960-1962.

The Reverend H. H. WALSH, M.A., S.T.M., PH.D. Professor of Church History, Faculty of Divinity, McGill University, Montreal. Author of *The Concordat of 1801* (1933) and *The Christian Church in Canada* (1956). Editor of the *Anglican Outlook*, 1950-1959.

FOREWORD

PROFESSOR DAVID W. HAY
Secretary of the North American Section
Faith and Order Commission on Tradition and Traditions

If the purposes of this volume are to be rightly appreciated, they must be seen in the context of a larger discussion which took its rise at the Third World Conference on Faith and Order at Lund in 1952. At that time it was widely felt that the comparative, phenomenological study of the agreements and disagreements of the churches had yielded all the profit that in the meantime could be expected. Even the adoption of a refinement proposed by Karl Barth of looking for the agreements in the disagreements and the disagreements in the agreements had led to little more than a tabulation of the status quo.

The Lund Conference decided that since the relation between Christ and his church is the foundation of everything, a study of this relation, cutting loose from prevailing differences and resorting to scriptural sources illuminated by the christological decisions of the great councils, gave most promise of reaching beneath ecclesiastical divisions. A special study commission on "Christ and His Church" was thereupon set up, and it rapidly became the major contemporary enterprise of the Faith and Order Commission.

Without questioning the value of the new study, Dr. A. C. Outler and Father Georges Florovsky urged at the same time that a historical study of the development of Christianity was inescapable, for realism demands that we deal with the churches in their concrete, empirical existence. Without historical investigation it is impossible to understand the present diversification of Christianity or to affirm with any credibility that there is despite our differences a common tradition that unites us all. The two scholars named were asked to report to the Faith and Order Commission when it would meet at Evanston in 1954 upon the advisability and feasibility of a special historical study. In consequence of their favourable report, a further study commission was set up, with a section in Europe and a section in North America, upon the subject "Tradition and Traditions." Dr. Outler was made chairman of the North American Section, Father Florovsky vice-chairman, and Dr. D. W. Hay secretary. The Canadian churches have been more fully represented than they might justly claim in the work of this section, in the persons of Dr. E. R. Fairweather, Dr. G. B. Caird (now in England), Dr. H. H. Walsh, Dr. D. M. Mathers and the secretary.

An interim report of the work of both sections of the Commission on Tradition and Traditions, along with one from the closely parallel Commission on Institutionalism, was published by the Student Christian

Movement Press in 1961 with the attractive title *The Old and the New in the Church*. The terms of the original proposal are there quoted (p. 12).

> We propose the establishment of a Theological Study Commission to explore more deeply the resources for further ecumenical discussion to be found in that common history which we have as Christians and which we have discovered to be longer, larger and richer than any of our separate histories in our divided churches.

The North American Section has experienced a sharp cleavage of views. Some members, insisting that the subject must be approached in a purely undogmatic, historical way, have urged that the proliferation of Christian divisions and the highly pluralistic form of their manifestation in the United States render the idea of a common history shared by all an illegitimate concept. "The Christian Tradition," if there ever was such a thing, has been dissipated in the relativities of history. Others have urged that "The Tradition" contains a suprahistorical dimension operating among the historical relativities and that therefore the idea of a "common history" is not only legitimate but necessary.

The work of the North American Section (as contrasted with the European Section, which has tended to concentrate more on the dogmatic issue of the relation of Scripture and tradition) has consisted of case studies in different periods of what Christians have believed about tradition and of how in fact it has operated among them, for example, in the ante-Nicene church, in the period of the great councils, in the continental Protestant Reformers, in Anglicanism to the Restoration, in the British Reformed churches, in the nineteenth century in Europe, and in the American churches. The section came to see that study ought also to be made of what happened to the European traditions as they were transplanted to the New World and of how these traditions were again modified as they were planted in Africa and the East by both European and American churches.

When the North American Section turned its attention to the Christian history of its own continent, it discovered that the Canadian scene could not be depicted with colours or media that would be appropriate to the United States. While these two nations have much in common, they differ markedly in their external relationships and in their internal histories —and not least in the manner of their confrontation of one another. The section had commissioned Dr. H. H. Walsh to work on the transmission of the Christian tradition in Canada, but it soon saw that the Canadian situation is so distinctive as to deserve intensified and extended study by a separate team of scholars. It therefore strongly encouraged Drs. Walsh and Hay to organize a group of Canadian historians who would undertake such a study, maintaining liaison with the section but working independently of it. This symposium is the fruit of their work. The results are factual and historical, but they are intended to illuminate the question how far the Canadian churches have "a common history" that is "longer, larger and richer than any of our separate histories."

Until fairly recently, the reunion of the Christian church has been sought chiefly through the comparative method. Negotiators have treated the various communions as so many independent entities, alike in some respects and different in others. Given this assumption, their task has been to reconcile the differences while taking advantage of the similarities. They have been chagrined to find that cataloguing disagreements does nothing to remove them. Disconcertingly perhaps, but not surprisingly, even well-meaning Christians often react to the discovery of differences by rallying to their own denominational standards.

Since about 1952, as Professor Hay as described, Faith and Order explorations have consisted mainly of attempts to outflank these set confessional positions. Theologians have been returning to the basic themes of the gospel to see if studying them together will put our varied emphases into a truer perspective. Historians, long relatively inactive in ecumenical discussion, have begun the study of "Tradition and Traditions" of which this symposium is a part.

The historians point out that the comparative method assumes that denominations are static and irreducible whereas in fact they are all products of history, owing their origin and their development to insights and movements, inspired people and charismatic groups. They further point out that Christian communions are all in some measure products of a common history, owing their ultimate origin to the same historic events, the same basic interpretation of these events and the same descent of the Holy Spirit. They urge, therefore, that reunion be approached not merely as an exercise in problem-solving but as an attempt to rediscover and to re-establish a common history.

The study of tradition has two aspects. On the one hand, it invites us to judge our separate traditions by referring them back to the common history—that is, the common experience—upon its relation to which every church bases its claim to be recognized as Christian. On the other hand, it attempts a cross-fertilization of traditions by seeking out what the Holy Spirit was saying to the whole church in the various movements that have hardened into exclusive denominations. It does not evade our differences, but in the manner of historians it approaches them in terms of how they came about and sometimes of how and where they went wrong. It asks of us an unaccustomed sympathy in appreciating the historical significance of other communions and an unaccustomed severity in recognizing the historical relativity of our own.

Will this new method contribute significantly to the ecumenical discussion? It will certainly not resolve the theoretical difficulties, if for no other reason than that its basic method is not that of asking theoretical questions. But it may help to create a climate of mutual understanding, and by leading us to open our past histories to one another it may enable us to begin making a common history once more. There are hopeful signs, indeed, that in ecumenical dialogue we are already beginning to enjoy the sharing of experience that makes possible a common history as Christians.

This volume is an attempt to apply the approach through history to the experience of the Canadian churches. It is offered as a distinctively Canadian contribution to the Fourth World Conference on Faith and Order at Montreal. As an illustration of a particular method of ecumenical discussion it must be preliminary and tentative, but it may well prove useful also as a comparative study of the Canadian variations of the Christian tradition.

The original suggestion for this study in depth of Canadian church traditions came from the Theological Study Commission on Tradition and Traditions (North American Section) of the Faith and Order Commission of the World Council of Churches. The book itself is the work of Dr. David W. Hay, who conceived the basic design of the project; of Dr. H. H. Walsh, who assembled and supervised the team of writers; and of the authors of the various essays. My function has been the limited one of editing the manuscripts in Dr. Hay's absence from Canada and seeing them through the press.

John Webster Grant

THE CHURCHES AND THE CANADIAN EXPERIENCE

1

TRADITIONS OF THE CATHOLIC CHURCH IN FRENCH CANADA

MARCEL DE GRANDPRÉ

I

A rapid glance at my family tree shows me that my ancestors came from many of the French provinces although a large number came from Paris. Hundreds of branches stem from marriages performed in Canada between 1633 and 1700, very few from marriages after that date. An ancestor of mine came from Ireland and was married here in 1670, another from Scotland in 1714. An ancestress came from England before 1700, while another, captured at Deerfield, Massachusetts, in the expedition of 1704, did not return home when she was freed but preferred to found a home in the land of her conquerors.

The fact that my ancestors came from twenty-nine of the provinces of France helps to explain the great diversity among the colonists of New France. In the seventeenth century there was no common language in the provinces of France, and their traditions were equally varied. There were about three hundred systems of customary law over which the royal power had very little control.

In Canada, however, where they arrived in small groups and scattered quickly over a large area, the colonists were compelled by force of circumstances to adopt a single language to which each part of France made its own contribution. There was only one legal system, the customary law of Paris. In language and in law the Canadian colony knew a unity that never existed in France before the Revolution.

Recruitment for the colony was carried on by the Notre Dame Society of Montreal under the direction of the Sulpicians, and by the Jesuits. With these two groups we find ourselves at the very heart of a great spiritual revival that had an extraordinary influence on seventeenth-century France. The reforms decreed by the Council of Trent were never accepted by the parliaments of France. It was only because of the fervour of some of her members that the church of France was able to renew herself, for the initiative was not taken by any decree of church or state.

Mgr. François de Montmorency-Laval was a pupil of the Jesuits. Right from the beginning Richelieu had determined that only Catholics would be admitted to New France, thus saving the colony from the politico-religious quarrels of the mother country. My paternal ancestor, together with his mother and his two sisters, sailed from La Rochelle on April 16, 1658, when he was only sixteen. They had been Calvinists, but abjured their beliefs before they set sail. The struggles of Jansenism, no less political than religious, found hardly an echo in Quebec, and the same was true of Gallicanism. The kings generally supported the bishops and the religious communities, and allowed both to establish closer contacts with Rome than the church even in France was allowed to make.

From the beginning, then, in marked contrast to old France, the population was united by language, by law and by religion. The habitants very soon came to have a common outlook and to regard as foreigners those who arrived from France in the service of the king and had no intention of staying permanently. In their own eyes, the habitants were the only true "Canadians."

From the tales of the missionaries, everybody in France knew about the life and the habits of the Indians, and about the difficulties encountered in converting them to Christianity and to the European way of life. Everybody knew about the risks involved in crossing the Atlantic—nearly always fatal for one person in five—and the rigours of the Canadian climate. New recruits were therefore not very easy to find. Under these conditions a person had to be physically strong and have a keen desire for adventure to leave a beautiful and well organized country. The main compensation was that he could find in Canada a land of wide open spaces, a veritable empire to add to the Kingdom of France, so many places to settle that it was difficult to choose from them all, and a fertile soil that only needed to be cleared.

Fate decreed that France, the first power in Europe, should be continually at war with some "soldier" who was generously subsidized by England, her arch-rival. It was never possible to mobilize the large amounts of capital that would have enabled a large population to be brought to Canada and thus to create a market. For lack of a market, the admirable efforts at organization that were made by Talon as early as 1672 were doomed to produce no result. Both industry and agriculture, even in their early stages, were already producing more than the population could consume. Trade with the French West Indies was never very profitable, for they could find a more lucrative market in New England. The chief market in France was for furs, but these were often in competition with furs imported from Russia. The upshot was that the colony produced only things that were already plentiful. Every year the intendant paid the public accounts with promissory notes that were immediately handed over to the merchants in return for their wares. The following spring the money that arrived from France was paid out to the merchants, who in turn sent it back to France for goods poured into their warehouses.

A people without money, the colonists had to shift for themselves in order to live. The land cost nothing. The siegneur, a kind of land agent, was obliged to give land freely in return for a rent that was little more than symbolic. Compelled to provide expensive public services, he had limited powers somewhat similar to those of a modern municipality and more often than not he was hard up. Living very close to his tenants, he was frequently a junior officer who had settled in the country or a native who had done well enough to buy up a seigniory. Next to the seigneur was the captain of militia, a native elected by his peers, who was in charge of the shooting practice of all the able-bodied men on Sundays. It was he who passed on the decisions of the Crown, the governor and the intendant. To these we may add the churchwardens, also elected, and responsible with the parish priest for the physical aspects of the religious life of the area.

All these leaders had places of honour in the church and were very touchy about questions of precedence. But the undoubted head was the priest, himself a Canadian. At the beginning, the population was scattered along the waterways in small settlements, and each missionary had to serve a large territory, travelling from one place to another and putting up at one of the houses where he said Mass. As soon as the settlement was large enough, it built a small church and then a presbytery, and an effort would be made to obtain a resident priest. The priest was charged with the care of all the souls in the parish. On Sundays, the parishioners put on their best clothes and went to church for Mass and sermon. The children went to catechism in the afternoon, often accompanied by their mothers and grown-up sisters, while the men discussed the latest news and bought what they needed for their farms. During the week the children were made to repeat their catechism and daily prayers were said in every home. The priest visited each family four times a year so that he knew personally every one of his parishioners and their problems, saw every child grow up and trained him.

II

The doctrinal basis of this way of life may be found in a volume, *Le Catéchisme du Diocèse de Québec*, written by Mgr. de Saint-Vallier and published in 1702.[1] In its 537 pages we find, first of all, a résumé of the great biblical narratives with detailed references to the biblical texts. Then comes a systematic explanation, in question and answer form, of Christian doctrine backed by biblical references. This is followed by teaching on the meaning of fifty-nine of the holy days and of religious ceremonies. The last part contains a collection of prayers for all occasions: at the start of the day's work; grace before and after meals; at the striking of the clock; prayers for grace to fight sin and temptation; prayer at bedtime. For small children and those without a great deal of intelligence the work was also published in an abridged form, *Le Petit Catéchisme*.

The catechism was the tool by which the Canadian Catholic was shaped. Every child learned the shortened form at home long before there was any question of his going to school. All the stories of the Bible were told to him over and over again so that he was quite familiar with the Gospel narratives, the parables and the prayers that were said. He had seen people make the traditional

[1] A photographic edition has recently been produced in Montreal by *Les Editions Franciscaines*.

Christian gestures and had made them himself long before he was aware of their full meaning. Sayings and proverbs that expressed the wisdom of his people were frequently drawn from Scripture. His mentality was already Christian when he began to take his part in the activities of the family, to do the small tasks allotted to him, and to go to school.

Soon he started on the large catechism which, like the small manual, he learned at home. Towards the age of eleven he prepared for First Communion by spending two full months in the study of the catechism. The priest was responsible for his education during this period and gave him a review of the whole of Christian doctrine. The First Communion was an important event both in the family and in the parish; it marked a stage in the religious and social life of the communicant, for he now felt himself to be an integral part of his community.

Catechetical instruction played an important role in the whole Catholic Church at that time, but it was given a higher place in Quebec than anywhere else. The church was, indeed, the centre of both religious and social life. Parish boundaries were civil as well as religious lines of demarcation, and the parish priest, often the best educated person in the area, performed certain secular functions in addition to his religious ones. He thus became the counsellor *par excellence* in almost everything.

The expression "*institution catéchistique*" has been used to designate all the means by which this Christian mentality was transmitted.[1] On the merely human plane the catechism is a fine instrument for the training of the mind. The biblical stories are within the reach of the simplest minds that can take in concrete facts. The liturgical life is somewhat more subtle, for symbolism is its means of expression, but if a person is willing to take the time to grasp its meaning he enters a world as enriching for the mind as it is for the heart. Again, the catechism furnishes the mind with abstract formulas of great theological and philosophical precision that are used in the exposition of Christian doctrine. At first they

[1]Fernand Porter, O.F.M., *L'institution catéchistique au Canada, Deux siècles de formation religieuse, 1633-1833* (Montreal: Les Editions franciscaines, 1949), xxii-322 pp. It seems to me that nobody can truly understand the mentality of the French-Canadian Catholic without reading this book.

are stored in the memory, but over the years explanations of them are heard many times. They are heard on Sundays in the sermon. Above all, in the ups and downs of life, in joys and sorrows, marriages and bereavements, successes and failures, people turn to them for assistance in forming judgments and making rules for conduct, to receive encouragement and to find reasons for living. An abstract vocabulary of considerable length thus becomes over a period of time part of a person's being. The vocabulary itself, the methods of reasoning and the explanatory procedures are, of course, all drawn from scholastic philosophy. Nor is its use confined to religious thought alone. It enables a person to become more intellectually mature, more quick-witted and more capable of dealing with abstract problems. It helps to explain why the pastoral letters of our bishops have had such influence at critical moments in our history and why the priest could find happiness in living among people less well instructed than he, it is true, but soundly educated and ably equipped mentally. Travellers who came here were frequently struck by this fact.

III

It could be said that the influence of the catechism was no different here from anywhere else in the world or, on the contrary, that the influence of the priests gave to French-Canadians a narrow outlook, a docility of spirit and an instinctive clannishness. Such an opinion is denied by the facts.

The economic and political structure of Canada under the French regime was hardly likely to restrict to the narrow confines of a parish either the interests or the activities of a population descended from adventurous immigrants. French Canada stretched from the Gulf of St. Lawrence to the head of Lake Superior, from Hudson Bay to the Gulf of Mexico. French-Canadians lived in constant contact with large numbers of Indian tribes. Since the land required about six years of work before it yielded a regular harvest, it was necessary to find a source of income elsewhere. This was easy. Every year hundreds of men were needed for the fur trade, for the transportation of supplies to distant posts, and for various government missions. As soon as a boy felt strong enough to handle a paddle and carry a heavy pack on his back, he dreamed of renting his services. Every Sunday after Mass the *salle des habitants* of the smallest church echoed with the latest news from the four corners of a country that was a veritable empire. Diplomatic relations with the English colonies or the Indian tribes, climatic variations in distant regions, the smallest incident on a long expedition could mean anxiety or bereavement, happiness or misery in the most ordinary home. The attraction of great adventure and of quick profits made the hard and monotonous life of the farmer seem dull in comparison.

The study of the catechism taught a person to make Christian judgments on all the events of life. It gave him a liking for abstract ideas and developed in him a critical spirit. In the church the Canadian listened to his priest and on important occasions he went to consult him, but after Mass he did not hesitate to express his personal opinion, to discuss what he had come to hear. After having asked advice he often sulked or at least did not accept it until he had thought it over. What quarrels there were between priests and their parishioners, between neighbours, between parents, what discussions about the site and construction of a church, what interest in quarrels over precedence! How tempers flared in disputes over the sale of spirits or the smuggling of furs, to give only two examples! A fault of the Latin temperament, perhaps, but it soon made itself at home in Canada.

In seventeenth-century France the ownership of land was a token of security, even of wealth. Almost impossible to obtain in France, land was free in Canada. With a little courage and a pair of strong arms trees were cut and a home built, land was cleared and a fine farm was developed from which a family could get enough to eat even in the lean years. There was hardly any outlet for the sale of agricultural products, but with a little ingenuity the articles that normally had to be bought could be made at home. Preference was always given to the craftsmen among the French who volunteered to work for a Canadian for three or five years, and since a good number of these decided to settle in the country after their period of service was over, the little tricks of their trade soon became known on every farm. The habitant was a resourceful person and so able to supply the needs of his family without too much dependence on outside help. He had all the necessities and few expenditures. He made a virtue out of necessity and felt himself to be truly independent, his own master. He finally reached the point of having a few luxuries. He loved social gatherings that generated wholesome merriment. The clergy often complained about the excessive expenditures that resulted from his fondness for feasting and for clothes.

Even so, the habitant was strictly limited in his resources and would not have tolerated anyone who insisted that he had to help pay the cost of public services. The running of the country depended on the Court at Versailles, and it was from there that the money ought to come to carry out decisions made there.

The religious authorities (the bishops of Quebec, the superiors of the Sulpicians and the Jesuits) had very close but often strained relations with the governor and the intendant. It was usually easier for them than for the civil authorities to intervene at the Court, the length of their time in office and their knowledge of the country giving their words greater weight there. Their *modus operandi* also enabled them to develop well organized seigniories, almost the best, covering nearly a quarter of the land that had been tilled. The civil authorities maintained an attitude toward them that was at once deferential but firm. There was truly a union of church and state, though broken by innumerable quarrels. The marriage knew many tensions on the surface, but underneath was a profound harmony.

The Canadian Catholic of the French regime had the same religious make-up as Catholics of all time and of every country, but we may single out some superficial characteristics that gave him a different kind of look—a particular kind of face, so to say. The intensity of parish life taught the Canadian how to live and how to think. It did not prevent him from being interested in the vast country beyond, however, and anyone could realistically dream of commercial, civil or religious activities that might send him off to the end of a continent. He was deeply imbued with a Catholic philosophy of life, but he liked to make up his own mind and to criticize. He was not easy to convince. He loved to argue for the sheer pleasure of it, but he sometimes became a pettifogger. A corner of the earth belonged to him, and when things went badly he took refuge there and got out of his difficulty all alone. So he was independent, often individualistic and difficult to lead. He did not like the superior authority of the state to interfere in his personal affairs and make him share in the cost of public services. His religious leaders had considerable independence in their dealings with the representatives of the civil authority and enjoyed great prestige.

IV

The war that led to the British conquest quickly impoverished the Canadians. A great deal of their property was plundered and a large number of their homes destroyed. The cessation of hostilities was a great relief, for everyone could now go home and repair the damage. In the parishes daily life soon returned to normal. The new ruling class had money and paid for everything they bought in good hard cash. Final decisions now came from London instead of Versailles, but it was still the captain of militia, still elected by the local residents, who carried them out. The changes were not very noticeable, and there seemed to be no cause for alarm. Generally speaking, the new people in authority were well educated and appeared to be well disposed; personal contacts with them were not too unpleasant. Soon the English bought the seigniories and when they lived on them were found to be likeable and worthy of respect. This helped the French to forget certain less desirable qualities, haughtiness and lack of scruple, greedy merchants and officials whose power had gone to their heads.

On the English side it was difficult to reconcile the Act of Supremacy with the granting of liberty to the Catholic Church. In Canada and in London statesmen and jurists gave different opinions depending upon their personal inclinations and the political circumstances of the time. A compromise was finally reached by which the Canadians continued to live according to their lights and the English hoped to win back the concessions they had made.

For the Canadians, the conquest meant a falling back upon themselves in the narrow territory of a province of Quebec practically limited to the inhabited regions along the St. Lawrence. If a man took part in an expedition for purposes of trade or exploration, he felt that he was nothing more than a wage-earner in the service of a foreigner.

In 1791 they began to elect members to the legislature and became passionately interested in politics. A new type of person now appeared in French-Canadian life: the professional politician. The French-Canadian had always been against the government in the struggle for the control of finance, but he now found a way of becoming part of the government. A political vocabulary and philosophical ideas had been part of parish life, and the works of the French *philosophes* had found their way into Canada before the conquest. American propaganda had made him a bit of a rebel. His propensity for these new ideas enabled him to appear as an ardent patriot and at the same time, in the eyes of his priest, a free-thinker.

For a long time there was a dearth of men offering themselves for the priesthood. A great Christian revival took place during the era of Mgr. Ignace Bourget. In a few years priests were recruited in France, religious communities trained in France were brought to Canada, and orders founded in Canada knew a surprising success. The church in Canada offered Canadians what they had lacked since the Conquest, the possibility of dreaming in the dimensions of a continent. So they set out to win souls for Christ wherever they could find them in British territory right out to the Pacific. Indian languages were no more of a barrier than English or the distances that had to be traversed. The church had come into a new spring-time of the spirit, and her sun was shining again.

But it was no light thing for the Canadians to be governed by people of another language and another faith under laws and customs that were strange to them. They made a vain attempt to live a little outside the state and so to retain their independence in their parishes, but the texts of the laws, municipal regulations and contacts with Anglo-Protestants were bound to modify their out-look and their reactions to a certain extent. They got into the habit of thinking of the government as if it were a foreign one, yet they left to it the responsibility for public works as much as they possibly could. They distrusted it, perhaps, yet they thought it could get along by itself without dipping into the pockets of Canadians, so they let matters alone and continued as before. They bent their backs under regulations that were unacceptable to them, but when their patience was exhausted they reacted violently enough to make the government back down. They retained their habit of turning everything into a joke, so that the most violent discussions ended in laughter. They loved parties where they ate well and had a gay time with parents and friends. The parish priests found that they wanted too many clothes and too much spirits. The better-class English were, in comparison, dignified, serious-minded, hard working and temperate. Attitudes to sex among French-Canadians perhaps owe more to Anglo-Protestant Puritanism than to French Jansenism.

V

The most important event in the life of French Canada during this period was probably the passing of the British North America Act. Confederation gave to Canadians for the first time—for they continued to reserve this name to themselves—a government of their own, that of the province of Quebec. Through the now familiar British institutions they were at last able to direct the organized life of the state. Up to this time French-Canadian society had been mainly parochial; now it became provincial. As parochial, it had also been Catholic. The provincial government, however, was by law neither Catholic nor Protestant as a result of the long struggles of Protestants for freedom of religion. No one any longer wanted an established church.

The Catholic Church was now better organized. The population remained faithful to it; new parishes had to be created and dioceses divided. Religious authority was no longer vested in one bishop but in the House of Bishops. The provincial cabinet was non-confessional, but the large majority of its members, like almost all the rest of the population, was Catholic. In fact, "French-Canadian" and "Catholic" were almost synonymous terms. Yet the people continued to guard their freedom of speech. They usually attended church regularly, but there were times when they disagreed with their parish priests and did not hesitate to say so, at least among friends; the more daring said so on public platforms or in the newspapers.

Political life has always aroused the interest of French-Canadians. Oratorical contests and public controversies have been meat and drink to them, and a struggle between the parish priest and the laity (churchwardens, aldermen, mayors) or between the bishops and the government has been a banquet. No one can really understand the mentality of the French-Canadian Catholic without reading that captivating chronicle, *L'Histoire de la Province de Quebec* by Robert Rumilly.

French-Canadian social life has remained profoundly Catholic. Quebec governments have gladly proclaimed themselves to be Catholic in spite of the wording of the Constitution that assigns to them a more impartial role. They have excelled in the subtle art of which the British are past-masters: divide and rule. While it has been impossible to find a break in the solidarity of the cabinet, the church in each diocese has been an independent authority. When public opinion is aroused and—as in Latin countries—confused about questions that cross the border-line between religion and politics, the government usually removes them from public discussion and then finds a practical solution in a way that is authentically British.

The French-Canadian continues to dream of undertakings beyond his borders. Migration to western Canada or to New England has satisfied his desire for change and his apostolic zeal. Canadian Catholicism has, through its missionary activity, now spread itself over the British Empire and throughout the world.

The French-Canadian is by disposition an independent person, capable of exercising patience for a long time until the day comes when he decides that he has had enough. Devoted to his ideas, he is always divided by theoretical controversies. Deeply Catholic, he is, however, a quibbler and loves to criticize his priest to such an extent that he at times appears to be a little anticlerical. He thinks that the state and the church should listen to each other and should work together, yet he does not see himself as a part of the state. He looks to the state to do everything, yet he resents its interference and hates to pay taxes.

Is the Canadian Catholic Church truly marked by these characteristics? Do these generalizations have any validity? To what extent can it be said that the Canadian church is French-Canadian, and can it be rightfully described by the method that I have chosen? It would be difficult to answer these questions with unanswerable proofs.

I am tempted to say that the principal characteristic is attachment to Rome. We have already met this under the French regime. The British conquest completely broke the ties between the Canadian church and France and gave to the Holy See a still more exclusive supremacy. Directives from Rome have always enjoyed a singular prestige among French-Canadians. But can it be said that this is a trait peculiar to them?

2

TRADITION IN THE ANGLICAN CHURCH
OF CANADA

T. R. MILLMAN

Anglican theologians in the classical period of the sixteenth and seventeenth centuries had much to say about tradition as a source of religious authority. The principal strand in the closely knit fabric was held to be the canonical scriptures, or, as one might say today, the tradition written in scripture. This was believed to be the final source of authority for religious truth. As Article Six says: "Holy Scripture containeth all things necessary to salvation: so that whatsoever is not read therein, nor may be proved thereby, is not to be required of any man that it should be believed as an article of the Faith, or be thought requisite or necessary to salvation."

A perusal of Anglican apologetic writing of this period will show how deeply revered the early Fathers were, particularly those who lived before A.D. 500, with Jerome and Augustine among the latest. The writings of the Fathers were an armoury from which Anglican defenders of episcopacy and reformed doctrine drew many weapons. But again and again the Fathers were held to be inferior to scripture.

Included in tradition were the creeds and the decrees of the general councils. The three creeds, asserts Article Eight, ought to be received and believed "for they may be proved by most certain warrants of holy Scripture." Of the three, the Apostles' Creed was put first because it was believed to be complete in essentials, a perfect summary of the fundamentals of the Christian faith.

In a narrower sense, as, for example, in Article Thirty-Four, tradition was understood to include certain rites and ceremonies of the church. These latter traditions were held to be subject to revision, but by action of the church only, not by private judgment. From a practical viewpoint, the church could not perform its functions without the aid of these traditions, but they were viewed as being essentially provisional in nature. A fair statement of the inconvenience arising from hasty and unadvised change, combined with a declaration that "particular Forms of Divine worship" are "things in their own nature indifferent and alterable," is contained in the preface to the 1662 revision of the Book of Common Prayer.

To sum up, Holy Scripture, the writings of the early Fathers, the decrees of the councils of the undivided church, the creeds, and a large number of rites, ceremonies and customs based on scripture make up in their totality the tradition which was handed on by the primitive church, received by the reformed church of the sixteenth century, and in turn handed on by it to modern Anglicanism. It goes without saying that this corpus of tradition was by no means distinctively Anglican. Yet the Church of England did hold these essentials tenaciously and in a manner peculiar to itself. With little change the Anglican Church of Canada continues to maintain these traditions to the present day.

Both before and after the Reformation, *Ecclesia Anglicana* was closely linked with the state. In the Middle Ages this relationship with government left the church with scope for independent action, but when royal supremacy was imposed by the Tudors these ancient liberties were considerably circumscribed. By the Elizabethan settlement the Church of England took on the nature of a religious establishment which it retained throughout the growth of the empire and commonwealth and which it still retains. Historically the reformed Church of England has never been a "free" church, that is, a church free from state control. Its bishops are still officially appointed by the Crown, which means, in effect, the prime minister. Its prayer book cannot be revised without the consent of Parliament.

The character of an establishment was invariably attached to colonial Anglicanism wherever this was possible. In the American colonies Anglicanism was established in Virginia, Maryland, South Carolina, North Carolina and four counties of the royal province of New York. In 1758 the first provincial assembly of Nova Scotia passed a statute enacting "that the sacred rites and ceremonies of divine worship according to the liturgy of the Church established by the laws of England shall be deemed the fixed form of worship among us, and the place wherein such liturgy shall be used shall be respected and known by the name of the Church of England as by law established." Statutes with similar intent were passed in 1786 by the legislature of New Brunswick and in 1803 by that of Prince Edward Island. Although Instructions given to successive governors of Quebec referred to the Church of England in that province as the "established church," yet for obvious reasons it was never accorded such a status by act of assembly. From the Cession of 1763 the Church of England in Quebec was favoured by government, and eventually government salaries were paid to several of its ministers. In 1791, when the provinces of Upper and Lower Canada were erected, a large landed endowment was set apart for "a Protestant clergy." Financial aid and official recognition by the British government continued for a time to be offered to the Anglicans. The age of the Reform Bill shut off this source of supply from England, and the granting of responsible government led to a similar outcome in the Canadas. By 1854 recognition of Anglicanism as an established religion was withdrawn, as it had earlier been in the Maritime Provinces.

The Church of England has never been established or endowed in Newfoundland, although it had a superior status there as the church of the mother country. The same remark may be made about Anglicanism on the west coast. George Hills, first Bishop of Columbia (1859-1892), and Edward Feild, Bishop of Newfoundland (1844-1876), were pupils in the school of tractarian theology, for which the church, as a divine institution with Christ as its Head, felt no need for the support of government. Hence, happily, neither the farthest Atlantic and Pacific areas experienced any struggle between champions of free and established churches.

When the time came for Anglicanism to expand in the huge central area of British North America, the idea of establishment was never entertained. The Hudson's Bay Company did in fact accord more recognition to the Church of England than to Roman Catholics and Methodists, but not on the score of any strongly-held religious preference. The Church Missionary Society, responsible in large degree for evangelizing the native races and for organizing the church, was a voluntary society with no tendency to look to the Company, or later to the government, for more support or recognition than the nature and extent of its work warranted.

Hence in the Canadian scene Anglicanism first appeared as a

religious system closely linked with the state, a virtual part of its working. This tradition was eventually broken and the Church of England emerged a century ago as one body of Christians among many, in no better and in no worse position than others in relation to government. One vestige of the ancient prestige attaching to establishment still remains and may be termed traditional. It is felt by many to be appropriate that public observances in connection with events in which Canada and Great Britain have been closely bound up should be held in Anglican churches or cathedrals. Older churches especially, with their regimental banners and furnishings of historic interest, are fitting places in which to conduct services of national significance. The Anglican mind is strong on continuity and likes to worship in surroundings that recall the story both of church and nation.

Royal supremacy was closely intermeshed with Anglicanism for so long a time as to make it appear doubtful whether the church could maintain a strong or effective existence without it. Yet it early became apparent, as for example in eighteenth-century Scotland, that the episcopal system could at least survive even under persecution. In the nineteenth and twentieth centuries more and more branches of the Anglican communion have been disestablished with nothing but good resulting. It is of interest to inquire what traditional elements in Anglicanism enable it to flourish independently of such an official relationship.

One observer finds these elements appearing clearly before the Reformation, in the fourteenth century, when as a result of the Great Schism a new understanding of the source of religious authority began to challenge papal absolutism. Canonists developed from biblical and juristic ideas the theory that final authority rested in Christ's body, the church; that the organ for expressing that authority was the council; that authority is mediated through the church and the council and is exercised representatively by them. The conciliar movement failed, but its basic ideas passed into the Anglican tradition and were expounded by Richard Hooker in the later books of his *Laws of Ecclesiastical Polity*. Later Anglican apologists bypassed Hooker and studied the conciliar movement itself. J. N. Figgis wrote: "Broadly speaking . . . [conciliar] ideas, and those ideas alone form the raison d'etre of the Church of

England against Ultramontanism on the one hand and individualistic Protestant sectarianism on the other." It was the conciliar element in Anglican tradition, on this view, in British North America as elsewhere, which enabled churches formerly tied to the state to develop an independent life and to form the Anglican communion.[1]

It is unlikely that any reasoned theory of this type was in the minds of Canadian Anglican leaders of the mid-nineteenth century when their church was being disentangled from its state connection. Two facts stood out clearly before them. The first was that Anglicanism in the British North American colonies could no longer hold on to its privileged position as an establishment. The other was that Anglican episcopalianism could flourish even in the American republic. But is also likely that the traditional understanding of the nature of the church, and of each separate part as a microcosm of the great church, was operative in Canada as in other parts of the world in which the Church of England was developing into the Anglican communion. The distinction, as well as the close connection, between the Catholic church and its parts is given clear expression on the Prayer Book title page: "The Book of Common Prayer and Administration of the Sacraments and other Rites and Ceremonies of the Church according to the Use of the Anglican Church of Canada."

Set within this expendable framework of establishment, however, many institutions and practices were retained which in varying degrees represent the continuity of the church from early ages. Chief among these was episcopal government. From 1634 the Bishop of London had jurisdiction over ministers in foreign plantations. He extended his jurisdiction to the vast regions acquired by the British Crown in 1713, and he retained it in Nova Scotia until the appointment of Charles Inglis as Bishop of Nova Scotia in 1787. In the American colonies the anomaly of an episcopal church without a resident bishop persisted from 1607 to 1784, when Samuel Seabury was consecrated in Scotland as Bishop of Connecticut. But the situation was recognized as unusual and, by many, undesirable, through this long period. In British North America, Anglicanism

[1] Leicester Webb, *The Conciliar Element in the Anglican Tradition*, St. Mark's Library Publications, No. 2 (Canberra, 1957), p. 15.

has had an almost continuous existence in Newfoundland since 1700 and in Nova Scotia since 1710. In the latter province St. Paul's Church was opened in Halifax in 1750 and Anglicanism began to grow with vigour, particularly after the coming of the Loyalists. Yet for eighty-seven years, indeed much longer, Newfoundland lacked resident episcopal oversight, and Nova Scotia had no bishop of its own for seventy-seven years. Anglicanism came to the Red River in 1820, yet it had to wait for its first bishop for twenty-nine years, except for a visitation made by G. J. Mountain, Bishop of Montreal, in 1844. On the west coast the first continuous Anglican endeavour began at Fort Victoria in 1849, but only a decade passed before a bishop came.

During these periods of varying length when no dioceses had been set up and no bishops appointed, the episcopal tradition was maintained in matters which related to that office. Ordination was obtained in England. Confirmation was not administered, but small numbers were prepared for the rite and welcomed to the Lord's Table under a rubric added to the Prayer Book of 1662 that "there shall none be admitted to the Holy Communion until such time as he be confirmed or be ready and desirous to be confirmed." A kind of pastoral oversight of the clergy was kept by commissaries or officials. At no time did Anglicans contemplate adopting a presbyterian form of ordination such as William White proposed in 1782 in his celebrated pamphlet *The Case of the Episcopal Churches in the United States Considered*. Perhaps the most eloquent plea for the setting up of episcopacy in Canada was made by Bishop G. J. Mountain after his visit to the Red River. He wrote:

I feel, with an indescribable force, the necessity of establishing a Bishop in those territories. Perhaps I need not disclaim such an idea as that all the virtue of the Gospel is centred in the episcopate, because I happen to hold that Thorny office myself; but it is the Episcopal Church of England which is specially, distinctly and loudly called to occupy that open field.[1]

Although the episcopal succession, once established, has been maintained without interruption in Canada, the bishops themselves, especially in the nineteenth century, exhibited an "infinite variety." The first of the Canadian line, Charles Inglis, was unique in that he

[1] *Journal of the Bishop of Montreal* (London, 1845), p. 169.

had lived in the American colonies for nearly thirty years before his exile to England as a Loyalist in 1783. When he came to Nova Scotia in 1787 he made no effort to imitate the lord bishops of England, for he was aware that pomp and circumstance would not go down well in colonial surroundings. He went about his duties, as he wrote to Bishop Jacob Mountain of Quebec in 1794, "with as little noise and offence as possible," and he did not become a member of the legislative council of the province until twenty years had passed. The first Anglican Bishop of Quebec, on the other hand, attempted to pattern his episcopate on the English model, closely connected with government, and he never succeeded in adapting himself wholly to Canadian life. His son G. J. Mountain, in contrast, was entirely at home in Canada, and so was the humble and saintly Charles James Stewart.

John Strachan as archdeacon and bishop was in a class by himself. He was of humble birth, and although he lived in comfort he did not lose the common touch. He was a firm believer in an established church, but when the hope of setting up such a church proved illusory he produced a kind of victory out of defeat, so fantastic was his energy and so indomitable his will. The tractarian bishops were another type again, magnifying their office, yet at the same time exercising their powers with discretion. Still another type of bishop was William Carpenter Bompas, a man who paid little attention to the externals of his office even in matters of dress, but whose labours and journeys call to mind the Celtic missionaries of early medieval times. Robert Machray stands out as a kind of nineteenth-century revival of the prince bishop of long ago, a natural leader, an educator and an ecclesiastical statesman.

Both the eighteenth century in England and the twentieth century in Canada produced (and produce) episcopal stereotypes; the nineteenth century did not. Yet despite the great variety in ability, background and personality of these men the essential tradition was preserved unchanged. Even the substitution of election by synod in place of royal appointment made no difference to the carrying out of the office itself.

Great emphasis must be placed on episcopacy for the simple reason that in the Anglican system bishops are the bearers of tradition, guardians of the deposit. Canadian bishops by their consecration oaths are committed to maintain "the Doctrine, Sacraments and Discipline of Christ, as the Lord hath commanded in his holy Word, and as the Anglican Church of Canada hath received and set forth the same." They have not been always successful, for example, in banishing and driving away all "erroneous and strange doctrine contrary to God's Word," yet they attempt to pass on to others, unimpaired, the faith of the church and the ordering of the church as that faith and order has been entrusted to them.

Episcopal traditioning may be seen in the action of Charles Inglis in issuing fourteen injunctions to his clergy in Nova Scotia and Quebec in 1789. The clergy were enjoined, among other things, to observe the rubrics contained in the Book of Common Prayer, and the Canons of 1603; to preach regularly once a Sunday; to read divine service on Wednesdays, Fridays and Holy Days; to baptize children in church except in cases of necessity; to baptize conditionally in doubtful cases; to catechize children every Lord's Day especially in summer; to administer Holy Communion at Christmas, Easter and Whitsunday, and as often besides as may be convenient, and to have a monthly administration in Quebec and Montreal; to apply the money collected at the Offertory for relief of poor communicants; to appoint two wardens and a select vestry each year.[1]

A further example of collective episcopal traditioning is the set of minutes issued by a conference of bishops held in Quebec in 1851. Here the bishops called for diocesan synods with lay representation; for a provincial synod under a metropolitan; for a revision of the Canons of 1603; for an observance of Prayer Book formularies and adherence to the Thirty-nine Articles; for care in conducting marriages and keeping registers; for support of church schools and Sunday schools. They concluded by praising the voluntary system of church maintenance. These minutes illustrate the passing on of older traditions, and also the influence of newer ideas such as lay representation in synods, and voluntarism.[2]

In pre-synod days, and indeed long after, the episcopal Charge was an effective traditioning agent. Bishop Stewart in his Charge of 1826 stressed attention to worship, psalmody, preaching, teaching of church principles, a good personal example, baptism, catechizing,

[1]H. C. Stuart, *The Church of England in Canada, 1759-1793*, pp. 73-75.
[2]A. W. Mountain, *Memoir of G. J. Mountain*, pp. 292-299.

preparation for confirmation, visitation of the sick. Bishop Strachan in his Charge of 1844 gave plain and simple instruction on what would be called today liturgics, pastoralia and homiletics. In more recent times the Charge gives the bishop an opportunity to comment on affairs both ecclesiastical and secular, to promote schemes of his own, and to give direction to the thinking of his diocese. It is not as marked an instrument for traditioning as it once was, but it occasionally follows the earlier pattern and may always be used in this fashion if need should arise.

The Book of Common Prayer is an extremely potent element in maintaining a fixed tradition. Until 1918 the Prayer Book used by Canadian Anglicans was that of 1662. A further revision was ratified in 1962. But the limits within which such revising should be made were clearly set out by General Synod, "forbidding any change in text or rubric which would involve or imply a change of doctrine or principle" as set forth in the book of 1662. Lambeth Conference resolutions of 1908 and 1948 also act as a guide for prayer book revision. The current Prayer Book prints the Solemn Declaration made by the first General Synod in 1893 in which it is stated that members of that synod were determined to maintain the prayer book and to transmit its teaching unimpaired to posterity.

Canon law is also a powerful element in maintaining tradition. Bishop Inglis mentioned the Canons of 1603, and so did the Conference of 1851. When synods were developed, constitutions and canons were adopted for each. These present considerable variety, but a commission is even now working on the production of a uniform code for the Anglican Church of Canada.

The Canadian church, as may well be supposed, perpetuates the traditions of the Church of England. Indeed its popular name not long since was the "English Church." This tendency was strengthened, particularly in the last century and down to World War II, by recruitment of English clergy, immigration of English laity, and financial support from English missionary societies. For the first generation of English immigrants the church provided a cultural as well as a religious bond with the homeland.

The influence of the Church of Ireland on the Anglican Church of Canada is noteworthy. A large number of clergy, forced to leave their native land because of the tithe war in the 1830's and other circumstances, brought with them a sturdy Protestant conservatism that went far to oppose and counteract the Catholic influences of the Oxford Movement. The strength of the Irish element, both of clergy and laity, was clearly seen by the defeat of A. N. Bethune and the election of Benjamin Cronyn in the first episcopal election held in the diocese of Huron. Irish influence may be discerned in the founding of Huron College, London, the Montreal Diocesan Theological College, and Wycliffe College, Toronto. By no means all the Irish clergy were "low church" evangelicals. John Travers Lewis, graduate of Trinity College, Dublin, and first Bishop of Ontario, held many ideas in common with the revived churchmanship of the nineteenth century. By and large Irish churchmanship has exerted a conservative influence and has tended to suspect any change in ecclesiastical practice that seemed to look in a Romeward direction.

Scottish Episcopalians who emigrated to Canada were too few to make their influence felt. Such influence is, however, discernible in the life of John Strachan who carried with him enough of the non-juring tradition of his paternal ancestry to be undisturbed by Tractarianism, recognizing in it some of the familiar usages of the Episcopal Church of Scotland.

After the mother Church of England the Protestant Episcopal Church has had the strongest influence on Canadian Anglicanism. From this church came synods with lay representation, the Domestic and Foreign Missionary Society (1883-1902) and the woman's organization that was auxiliary to it. Down the years Canadian dioceses have kept watch on what the American church was doing in religious education and in missionary endeavour. American bishops have assisted at Canadian consecrations for over a century, and Canadian bishops have been in close touch with all movements in the American church. Clergy pass readily from one church to another. It is worthy of remark that the example of the Episcopal Church, powerful as it has been, has not had a greater influence on Canadian Anglicanism. English traditions, on the whole, have been held more strongly. An acute observer from overseas, on a recent visit to Canada, found the Anglican Church here "very English, conservative and stuffy!"

Because of its sectional and diocesan development, and because of the distinctive stamps placed on dioceses by founding bishops, many parts of the church have developed traditional modes of thought and action. Newfoundland, for example, only recently linked up constitutionally with Canadian Anglicanism, has been closely attached to the mother Church of England. The long episcopate of Edward Feild imparted to the diocese a quality of its own that was further emphasized by the church school system. The Newfoundland Anglican, other things being equal, is perhaps a better instructed churchman than his mainland contemporary. Nova Scotia and Fredericton churchmen have a tendency to be "stiff" in their opinions and to defend the faith with vigour. Anglicanism in the province of Quebec has a unique flavour. It does not fear the Church of Rome (or the French-Canadian), nor does it seek to mirror any of its great neighbour's ways. It has a deep un-selfconscious understanding of its own being. Ontario Anglicans present many regional differences, but because their church is strong in that province in terms of numbers and worldly wealth they have developed a kind of assurance, an expansionist mentality, a willingness to accept responsibility and to give leadership. The church of the mid-west, familiar with "boom and bust," has also, with all its variety, some common characteristics. Recent in origin, it is still a missionary church, and it bears the marks of the primitive simplicity and adventurousness of its founders. The church of the west coast, like that of the east, has preserved strong lines of communication with the Church of England. Anglicans of both coasts keep a watchful eye on the tendency to centralize the church's work in Ontario. Anglicanism works best, they seem to feel, when the individual dioceses, or at least the various geographical areas of Canada, preserve a strong dash of independence and local liberty. Of the church in the great north it is difficult to make any generalization, except to hazard the opinion that the unsophisticated Anglicanism produced in it is distinct in kind. Its Indian and Eskimo adherents are loyal to it not so much because they have chosen it out of a number of competitors as because it was the faith that brought the Gospel to them at the first. Yet, when all these differences are tabulated, and varying traditions isolated from each other, the Anglican Church of Canada is still one, or as much "one" as its historical origins and tensions permit.

3

THE CONGREGATIONAL TRADITION IN CANADA

EARL B. EDDY

I

The Reformation moved slowly in England, lacking a colourful and symbolic leader like Luther in Germany or Calvin in Geneva. In the absence of bold action by leaders of church or state the movement was pressed by the common people, who had grown restive at the lack of progress in the parish churches. Following the lead of the university centres, conventicles of dissenters arose in countless communities, and many books and tracts were published criticizing the church for her Romish practices and for the illiteracy and intolerance of her clergy. These dissenters were widely scattered but had much in common.

From their theory of church government they were called "Independent" or "Congregational." Presbyterians in Scotland held to the principle of the "equality of ministers," but they gathered clergy and elders into a "presbytery" to rule the church. The English dissenters gave all power of government, under Christ, to the local congregation. They supplemented this independence, however, by calling ministers and laymen together in "councils" to give advice, when asked, about the ordination, induction or discipline of the clergy. Later generations organized unions and associations to pursue the wider tasks of the church—the education of its ministers, missionary endeavour, the publication of periodicals, and relations with the state and with other denominations.

Doctrinally, the dissenters of England were akin to those in Scotland; indeed, history has shown that no less than five "Congregationalists" helped to frame the Westminster Confession, which was generally accepted by both English and American streams of Congregationalism as, in essence, their standard of faith.[1] But, recognizing the need for each generation to restate its creed in contemporary symbols, each local congregation (and indeed each larger council) was encouraged to formulate its own unique "confession of faith" and "covenant."

The principle of "the gathered church" was inherent in Congregationalism. Men and women who made public profession of Christ before the congregation were, upon vote of the people, admitted to "covenant-membership." Their spiritual development and their backslidings were subject to discipline by the congregation. Authority for such discipline was found in Matthew 18: 15-18. Great power was given the local church, both over the personal lives of its members and over its own corporate life, because dissenters held that "the decision of a meeting of believers, properly called, and invoking the Presence of God in His Holy Spirit, was in reality, the Voice of God."[2] Those who for personal reasons could not make public profession of their faith posed a problem for Congregationalism at the very outset. Many of them were in sympathy with the aims and purposes of the church but felt themselves unable, or unworthy, to take that step; these frequently outnumbered the covenanting membership.

The officers of a congregation varied slightly in different traditions, but all were of New Testament origin. The followers of Robert Browne elected "Pastors, Teachers, one or more Elders, one or more Relievers, and one or more Widows," while those who were influenced by Henry Barrowe confined the list of officers to "Elders and Deacons." None would follow Calvin so far as to have the elders constitute a session.

Freedom from state control was essential to the spirit of Congregationalism. It was an ideal much to be desired in the middle of the

[1]Savoy Confession (England, 1658), in R. W. Dale, *A History of English Congregationalism* (London: Hodder and Stoughton, 1907), p. 363. Cambridge Platform (New England, 1643), in Leonard Bacon *et al*, *Ancient Platforms of the Congregational Churches of New England* (Middletown: Edwin Hunt, 1843), pp. 74-148. Saybrook Platform, based on the Cambridge, in Bacon, *op. cit.*, pp. 153-241.

[2]From an unpublished thesis by the writer, "The Beginnings of Congregationalism in the Early Canadas," 1958, in the Victoria University Archives, p. 300, which acknowledges debt to Dale, *op. cit.*, p. 121.

sixteenth century, when conventicles were proscribed and their members persecuted, imprisoned and even martyred. But two centuries later, in more felicitous circumstances, this fair ideal was compromised; in Massachusetts and Connecticut, indeed, Congregationalism became a state church.

The relations of Congregationalism with other church bodies also varied. Browne had said:

The Church of England is inwardly corrupt, and outwardly under subjection to an unscriptural hierarchy, so that every Christian ought to strive to obtain its reform at once, or failing that, to separate from it to follow Christ.

There is no hope of reform for the Church of England from the civil power.

It is equally evident that no reasonable hope of reform is offered by the Presbyterian Plan.[1]

Barrowe, on the other hand, influenced by Calvin, and perhaps even more by Henry Jacob, one of the moving spirits behind the Millenary Petition, could not "rend the seamless garment of the Church." He claimed that there was a distinction between the "substance" of the church and a multitude of secondary accretions. He recognized the Church of England therefore as a true church, and persuaded John Robinson, the father of the Pilgrim Fathers, to renounce separatism. One of Robinson's followers expressed the position thus:

We will not say, as the separatists were wont to say on leaving England, "Farewell Babylon," but "Farewell to the Church of God in England." We do not go to New England as separatists from the Church of England, though we cannot but separate from the corruption in it.[2]

The Congregational ideal of return to the simplicity of the apostolic church as revealed in Scripture entailed also many lesser reforms: church architecture must be of the plainest sort—a bare meeting-house would suffice; ornateness of any kind, such as a

---

[1]Robert Browne, *Reformation without Tarrying for Anie*, quoted in Henry Dexter, *Congregationalism in the Last Three Hundred Years as Seen in its Literature* (New York: Harper, 1880), pp. 97-109.

[2]Francis Higginson on leaving England, quoted in Williston Walker, *A History of the Congregational Churches in the United States* (New York: The American Church Historical Society, 1894), II, 99.

stained-glass window or a carved altar, was summarily rejected along with vestments; the liturgy gave way to spirit-guided, spontaneous prayers; the pulpit, often raised to emphasize the importance of preaching, occupied the central place of the meeting-house; and the communion table, reduced to floor level in order to emphasize the equality and fellowship of the communicants, took the place of the altar.

II

It was nearly two centuries before the Congregational tradition reached British North America, two strands of it arriving in Nova Scotia almost simultaneously although by two strangely diverse routes. One came directly from England, where, over the years, it had followed Robert Browne's lead and had become known as the "Independent" Church. The other had been transplanted, first to Leyden under John Robinson, and later to New England, where it was called "Congregationalism." This tradition followed Henry Barrowe. Both strands had been altered by the exigencies of time and circumstance.

The Independent tradition had undergone the least change. Remaining on its native soil, surrounded by the larger Established Church, and always a minority movement, it had settled down from its earlier radicalism into a staid conservatism. Holding fast to its principle of freedom from state control, and holding itself somewhat aloof from its larger neighbour the Church of England, it prided itself on its freedom of prophesying. It developed notable pulpit orators, whose stature relieved it from the stigma of being called a "sect" and gave it denominational status.

It was natural that this Independent Church should develop men of adventurous spirit. In 1749, when the Honourable Edward Cornwallis called for pioneers to found a new colony at Halifax, the majority of the volunteers were members of the dissenting churches, "seven-eighths of them of the Independent tradition."[1] The governor immediately set aside lands and funds, not only for the Established Church, but also for the dissenters. St. Paul's was opened on September 2, 1750, and the dissenters' chapel, later known as

[1]Ian F. Mackinnon, *Settlements and Churches in Nova Scotia, 1749-1776* (Montreal: Walker, 1930), p. 72.

Mather's Meeting-house, in the following March.[1] It is significant, however, that the first minister of the meeting-house was from the American colonies. Thus the two strands, Independency and Congregationalism, met at the very beginning of the colonization of British North America. For a year or two the Independent tradition was in control, but it was swamped by the arrival of two thousand settlers from New England between 1749 and 1752.[2]

The Congregational strand had undergone a double transplantation, first to the Low Countries, and then to the new world of the American colonies. Arriving a hundred strong in the little *Mayflower* in 1620, they were to be reinforced in the next decade by the coming of other ships carrying members of their faith. But it was not until 1629, when the Massachusetts Bay Colony was founded at Salem, that there was any hope of success to this North American venture. Thousands of immigrants arrived in the next ten years, most of them members of, or friendly to, the Congregational Church, and thirty churches of that faith were organized.

Here, in the New World, Congregationalism was free to grow as it willed. It was the majority religion, the dominant religion, indeed for many years the only religion, somewhat intolerant of others. Before long it was powerful enough to become the established church in two of the larger colonies. In this favoured position certain features of the tradition were so emphasized and enlarged as to make it quite distinctive from the Independent strand of England.

1. Following Barrowe, three or more elders were appointed—a preaching elder, generally recognized as the minister; a teaching elder, charged with the responsibility of biblical and catechetical instruction; and a ruling elder, who was the business leader of the congregation and presided at official meetings of the church and congregation. This emphasis upon the importance of the eldership has led some historians to call the New England strand an "Independent Presbyterian Church" instead of using the better-known term "Congregational."[3]

[1] T. B. Akins, *History of the Settlement of Halifax* (Halifax: Herald Publishing Co., 1895), p. 21.

[2] Journal of the Board of Trade, Halifax, in the Provincial Archives of Nova Scotia, p. 391.

[3] Leonard Bacon, *The Story of the Churches* (New York: Baker and Taylor, 1904), p. 28.

2. A covenant, distinct and unique in each church, was framed and signed by members of the congregation. This requirement kept the faith fresh and alive by translating belief into contemporary symbols.

3. Discipline of members was strict and sure. It was at first exercised by the congregation in the public meeting but gradually was relegated to the minister and one or more elders, who acted on behalf of the people.

4. The congregation became divided into two parts, the "church" and the "society." The former was composed of covenanting members, who alone could discuss and decide spiritual matters—the calling of a minister, the framing of a covenant or confession of faith, the disciplining of a member. The latter included those who were in sympathy with the aims of the church and supported it financially, but who for personal reasons were unable to covenant together. The society handled all financial matters, holding property in trust, setting and collecting the minister's stipend, and in many cases undertaking the civil government of the community.

III

The Maritime colonies of British North America were soon to feel the weight of Congregationalism, not only in Halifax, where this tradition so quickly swamped the Independent strand, but along the shorelines of Nova Scotia, which were also settled predominantly by New England Congregationalists. Following Governor Lawrence's Proclamation of November, 1758, promising free land and freedom of worship to all Protestants, thousands of New England fishermen and farmers responded.[1] Chester was the first to be settled, in 1759. Then followed, in order, Liverpool, Cornwallis, Annapolis, Granville, Barrington, Jebogue, Sackville, Amherst and Cumberland by the end of 1761. Most of these groups brought their own Congregational ministers with them or elected one of their own number to lead them. Thus by 1761 Congregationalism was firmly established. It had built its own meeting-houses, called its own ministers, elected

[1]Maurice W. Armstrong, *The Great Awakening in Nova Scotia* (Hartford: American Society of Church History, 1938), p. 21. Eighteen hundred settlers arrived in 1760. In the first provincial census of 1776, out of a population of 13,374, there were 6,913 Americans.

its elders and deacons, divided its followers into church and society, and disciplined them for their many lapses. With the constant reinforcement of immigrants from their home colonies, the future looked bright for Congregationalism.

But the picture soon changed, and changed radically! Poverty was the first problem to make its impact upon these little churches in the new land. Most of the settlers were hard pressed from the very beginning. They had invested their ready cash in a minimum of farm equipment; but they still had to build houses and barns, clear, stump and fence the land, and dike the marsh, before any return was possible. Then only could they consider the community responsibilities of a saw-mill, a grist-mill and a church. The general expectation of a minister in the outposts was £80 a year, but few churches were able to pay it: Jebogue had averaged £25 for the first six years, and Chester even less.[1] A fund was started in Halifax for the relief of dissenting ministers. Its appeal was twofold: to the New England churches whence they had come, and to the older churches in England. Some measure of success rewarded their efforts, especially among their former friends. But the appeal to England was doomed from the start. A Halifax minister generously offered to go to England to solicit funds, but in May, 1770, after the King had donated £1,000, he disappeared, and with him all accounting of the monies collected.[2] Nevertheless the needy ministers did obtain some relief from the fund, generally about £40 each. It can be readily understood how difficult it would be to obtain and hold ministers under such impoverished conditions, when the general salary level in New England was above £150. Even Mather's Meeting-house in Halifax suffered greatly, and after being without a settled minister for more than thirty years, finally appealed to the Church of Scotland for help. A minister was sent out by that church, and before long Mather's Meeting-house became St. Matthew's Presbyterian Church.

The Congregational tradition in Nova Scotia suffered further because of the American Revolution. More than half of the New England settlers, and all but two of their ministers, returned to their

[1]Records of the Church of Jebogue, typescript copy in the Provincial Archives of Nova Scotia, pp. 96-98.
[2]*A Brief State of the Circumstances of the Dissenters in Nova Scotia*, in the *Nova Scotia Documents*, Vol. 284, No. 18, in the Provincial Archives of Nova Scotia.

old homes.[1] One minister who remained, the Reverend John Seccombe, was thrice tried for treason,[2] while two others only escaped a similar trial by precipitous flight.[3] Cut a church membership in half and leave it without ministerial leadership, and you make it a prey to any promising novelty. Add to this the question of whether it was not a mark of disloyalty to support a church that seemed wholly to belong to a power with which your country was at war, and you have a situation ripe for division.

Henry Alline proved to be the catalyst that ended the Congregational tradition in Nova Scotia. He had left New England as a boy of twelve when the "Newlight" movement was at its height. Uneducated, yet possessing a certain emotional fire, he made his appeal to the Cornwallis congregation in 1776. Some sixty or seventy members followed him to found the first "Newlight" body in nearby Newport, but he was far from satisfied. He began an "evangelistic" tour, dividing Congregational churches wherever he went and establishing his own congregations. Congregationalism was never to recover from this division, for most of his churches eventually became Baptist.

We come then to this conclusion: the Congregational tradition suffered eclipse in Nova Scotia because of its difficulty in securing ministers and an equal difficulty in supporting them from already meagre purses, because of the incursions of the Alline movement, and because of the loss of pastors, people and prestige at the time of the American Revolution. By the end of the eighteenth century the eleven churches of Congregationalism had been reduced to two struggling congregations, Jebogue and Barrington.

IV

The dissolution of the Congregational churches of Nova Scotia disclosed a serious fault in their polity: the autonomy of the local congregation was a coveted tenet of church government; but coupled with it, and its complement, was the practice of summoning councils

[1] James Woodrow, in the *Canadian Independent*, Vol. XII, No. 12, p. 388.

[2] In 1771 while supplying the Halifax church with three of the church officials; also September 1, 1776, and June 1, 1777. R. M. Hattie, *Looking Backward over Two Centuries*, a souvenir of the 200th year celebration of St. Matthew's Church (Halifax, privately printed, 1949), p. 12.

[3] Rev. Benaiah Phelps of Cornwallis and Rev. Seth Noble of Maugerville.

for advice upon matters relating to the ministry and the larger work of the church. Both of these principles must obtain if Congregationalism is to be effective.

The use of councils to enrich congregational independence was a proven instrument in England, although there they were always summoned for a stated purpose and dissolved upon its accomplishment. In New England, with its more than five hundred Congregational churches, councils had also proven themselves and had been provided with a somewhat more permanent structure. But in Nova Scotia, where churches were often a hundred miles apart and means of communication intolerably slow, councils of churches for mutual help and understanding were impracticable. Ministers were called and inducted, resignations offered and accepted, problems relating to clerical discipline settled, without so much as sending out letters-missive to call a council. Indeed, only one council met in the first half-century of Congregationalism in Nova Scotia; that council was held in 1770 at the request of the Dutch Calvinist Presbyterian Church of Lunenburg for the purpose of ordaining its pastor. Thus one can understand that the Congregational churches, utilizing only half of the strength of their basic polity, were not able to withstand the many inimical pressures, and in the end succumbed to the more flexible Baptists.

A half-century after the meeting-house in Halifax was opened, a similar experiment was tried in Quebec City with similar results. It became clear, therefore, that stronger ties with one or other of their bases must be made before Congregational stability could be assured. It would have seemed natural to strengthen the link with New England because of her geographical proximity. Between 1776 and 1812, however, relations between Britain and the United States were never entirely cordial, and with the outbreak of hostilities in 1812 they deteriorated still further.

Canadian Congregationalism, divided and shattered, now turned to England for succour. Henry Wilkes, a young apprentice in Montreal, was destined to play a large part in effecting this bond. Born in England of Independent stock, he had emigrated to Canada with his parents in 1819. In 1827 the Canada Education and Home Missionary Society, composed of Presbyterian, Baptist and Congregational representatives, was organized in order to aid needy charges and to secure ministers for them from the Old Country. Wilkes was named secretary from the beginning, so that he was immediately put in touch with the missionary societies of England and Scotland.

When Wilkes went to Glasgow to study for the Congregational ministry, the Canada Education and Home Missionary Society commissioned him to seek out men for the churches in Canada, and he was successful in enlisting three men in his very first year. The London Missionary Society gave £1,000 to the work, which enabled him to secure more men for Canada; and in 1836 the London Missionary Society organized a subsidiary, the Colonial Missionary Society, to foster this work on the frontiers.

After a three-years' pastorate in Edinburgh, Mr. Wilkes was called to a newly founded Congregational church in Montreal; at the same time he was appointed agent for the Colonial Missionary Society in Canada. The double invitation seemed to be the call of God. He arrived in Montreal late in 1836 and immediately made a tour of the struggling Congregational causes in Upper and Lower Canada. He was so impressed with the possibilities that he asked the Colonial Missionary Society for a second agent to undertake the work from Kingston west, while he concentrated on the remainder of the two colonies. The request was granted and Mr. Wilkes was instrumental, directly or indirectly, in the establishment of at least twenty-five Congregational churches in the area under his direction. Nor did he forget the other part of his task, for an equal number of men were secured from England and Scotland to serve the new causes. At the end of 1841 the Colonial Missionary Society was aiding thirty ministers in Canada East and West.

Through its connection with the Colonial Missionary Society, the Canada Education and Home Missionary Society took on a strong Independent flavour, and gradually the other denominations withdrew to pursue their own work. This led to the organization of the Canadian Congregational Home Missionary Society to replace it. While continuing its direct connection with the Colonial Missionary Society, this new body found fraternal and financial help from the American Congregational Home Missionary Society. Canadian Congregationalism was now receiving aid from its parent strands in both England and New England.

Under this double parentage, Congregationalism flourished in the Canadas, and scores of charges were opened with an adequate supply of ministers. A Congregational college was organized to train its ministers. A periodical, the *Harbinger* (later the *Independent*), took its place among Canadian periodicals and kept the growing church informed of its successes and its hopes. The larger work of the church prospered, and the earlier weakness of Congregationalism seemed to be overcome.

V

The two streams of Congregationalism both fertilized the reborn Congregational churches of Upper and Lower Canada. English Independency was strengthened by thousands of immigrants of that faith, among them men of some stature. But the proximity of a powerful New England church was an influence not to be denied. The earlier churches of Nova Scotia had brought with them their home-name for the church, Congregationalism, and the term prevailed throughout all of the colonies. Yet this new frontier faith was able to select the best features of its twofold parentage and, in the end, to form a unique and indigenous Canadian Congregational church.

The English custom of using *ad hoc* councils seemed insufficient for the frontiers, where isolation and lack of communication required a closer fellowship. The American structure of associations of ministers, consociations of ministers and lay representatives, which eventually grew into state councils and in the end a national council, appealed to the Canadian church. It formed the Congregational Union of Upper and Lower Canada, yet limited the power of the Union so that it held only an advisory relation to the local congregation.

In other respects, too, Canadian Congregationalists blended and adapted the traditions of their forebears. The discipline of members by the congregation was generally handled by the minister and deacons. As the New England emphasis on the eldership diminished, indeed, the diaconate became more and more powerful and assumed responsibility for spiritual as well as material matters. The American distinction of "church" and "society" disappeared altogether in Canada, where no responsibility for civil or community matters rested upon a church that was completely separate from the state.

VI

The Congregational churches in Canada, so successful in establishing their causes in Upper and Lower Canada, never seemed to make the same impact upon the prairies of western Canada. This failure was not due to a lack of initiative or funds. It resulted partly because Congregationalists were overshadowed by three larger denominations—the Church of England, the Presbyterian Church in Canada and the Methodist Church—but more especially because the Independent spirit expressed itself in another way. In many small towns of the West, "union" or "community" churches were organized, composed of members of all faiths but independent of any of the larger bodies. This desire to form one church, and one church only, caught fire. When The United Church of Canada was formed in 1925, no less than three thousand such congregations joined in the union. These were in many ways Congregational, and they were a considerable force in the new United Church of Canada.

These "union" churches, together with their Congregational brethren in eastern Canada, faced a radical change in polity within the United Church. Their cherished principle of autonomy had to yield to the powers of Presbytery, and their unhindered choice in the calling of a minister to the Settlement Committee. Yet time had been conditioning them for that change. The dissolution of the Congregational churches in the Maritimes had taught the necessity of a more careful oversight by some larger body. The Congregational Union was the first answer of the churches; gradually it had been given more and more power, and the 1925 consolidation caused little perturbation because of polity.

Nor did the Congregationalists experience in the new church any radical departure from their earlier doctrines. Each local Congregational church had created its own "covenant" and "confession," and although there was a great similarity in thought if not in wording in these documents (as though they had followed a common model), their divergences were probably as great as the differences among the doctrinal statements of the denominations entering union. One has only to study the doctrines set forth by the National Congregational Council in 1883, and compare them with the United Church Statement of Faith, to realize how akin they are. With the exception of

Article X in the Congregational statement *re* Church Polity, there is no clash whatsoever.[1]

The Independent and Congregational traditions had merged in Canada into a unique and indigenous Congregationalism. It had selected the better features of each of its parents, as they seemed to suit the newer frontiers of the colony. It found a powerful ally in the "union" churches of the prairies. And although it lost its denominational label when in 1925 it almost unanimously entered The United Church of Canada, it never lost its denominational flavour of independency, for in the larger body this has been broadened and enhanced.

[1]Quoted in S. N. Jackson, *A Handbook of Congregationalism* (Toronto: Congregational Publishing Co., 1894), pp. 171, 172.

4

THE PRESBYTERIAN TRADITION IN CANADA

N. G. SMITH

I

Presbyterianism was brought to the colonies of British North America by immigration from the American colonies and from the British Isles. Among the settlers who came to Nova Scotia after the founding of Halifax were numbers of Presbyterians from the New England states who petitioned, without much success, for ministers to labour among them. Among the United Empire Loyalists who came to the Maritimes and the upper province after the American Revolution there were, again, numbers of Presbyterians, ministered to either by military chaplains or by ministers of the Presbyterian churches from the dissident colonies. For three decades after the Revolution there was a fairly steady trickle of immigration into the upper province from upper New York and Pennsylvania. It is estimated that at the time of the War of 1812 eight out of every twelve residents of the upper province were of American origin. From this point onwards immigration from the United States decreased and immigration from the British Isles increased. New frontiers being opened up to the westward attracted American land-seekers more strongly than the British provinces. At the same time the disbanding of regiments after the Napoleonic wars, the Highland Clearances and economic distress in the British Isles impelled great numbers of Scottish and Irish families to seek to improve their lot in the British colonies of North America.

As a result of these circumstances Presbyterianism in the colonies of British North America acquired a strongly British flavour. Congregations in the Maritimes, along the north shore of the St. Lawrence and in the Niagara peninsula, which had been founded by

Presbyterian or Reformed ministers from the United States, were absorbed in a church that looked increasingly to the Presbyterian churches of the British Isles for additions to its ministry and membership.

II

In the early stages of their development, the isolation of the colonies of British America from one another was an effectual barrier to communication. It is startling to realize that it took William Fraser nearly a month and a half to get from Pictou, Nova Scotia, to London, Upper Canada, in 1834.[1] While his journey was lengthened by several misfortunes, the hazards encountered were not unusual. Until improved methods of transportation and the coming of the railroads made travel easier, the churches of the Maritime Provinces and those of the upper provinces were separated by a formidable geographical barrier.

Their similar isolation from the parent churches in the British Isles tended to make the colonial churches virtually independent bodies. The colonial churches had no formal representation in the courts of the parent bodies and did not consider themselves as being necessarily bound by their decisions. Presbyterian polity did not lend itself to close supervision over the affairs of the colonial churches. There was in the Presbyterian churches nothing comparable to the close supervision exercised by the British Wesleyans over the Methodist missions in the Maritimes. Deputations from the Scottish churches visited the colonial churches occasionally, but not with the intention of giving specific directions concerning their administration. Their visits were more in the nature of good-will missions to indicate the interest of the churches of the homeland in the welfare of the colonial churches. In a letter addressed to the Kirk Synod of Canada in 1844 the parent church stated:

The Church of Scotland has never claimed any authority, nor exercised any control over your Synod: neither has she ever possessed, nor desired to possess the right of any such interference.[2]

[1]Diary of William Fraser, 1834-1835, in *Transactions of London and Middlesex Historical Society*, part XIV, 1930, pp. 84-94.
[2]Minutes, Synod of Presbyterian Church of Canada in Connection with the Church of Scotland, 1844, p. 9.

In meeting emergencies as they arose, the presbyteries of the colonial churches often pursued courses that would have been considered highly irregular in Scotland. When the Presbytery of Truro united with the Presbytery of Pictou in 1817 to form the Synod of Nova Scotia, the uniting bodies carried on their negotiations, consummated their union, and then informed the parent churches in Scotland of what they had done. In informing them of their action, they stated that they considered it a happy circumstance that in Nova Scotia there was no foundation "for those local controversies which have occasioned separation and division in Scotland." Such independence of action, necessitated by their isolation and the exigencies of frontier conditions, imposed some modifications upon the inherited traditions of the colonial churches.

Many of the first congregations in the British provinces were organized by ministers of the Secession churches which had broken away from the Church of Scotland in disputes that had arisen in Scotland over the relationships between church and state. Between 1690 and 1900 at least thirteen such divisions occurred among the Presbyterians of Scotland, either by secessions from existing groups or by the refusal of minorities to enter unions with their brethren. Most of these groups were small, but because a high level of piety and missionary zeal was maintained in them they often had a surplus of ministers. It was natural that these men should seek employment among their countrymen in British North America. Churches established by these Secession ministers were Presbyterian in doctrine, government and worship. Because of the great scarcity of ministers in the colonies, "Kirk Folk" of the Church of Scotland were often content to accept the ministrations of Secession ministers.[1] Being already accustomed to the voluntary method of church support, these ministers were in many ways better able to adapt themselves to the colonial situation than were the ministers of the Church of Scotland. Ministers of the Kirk were understandably reluctant to give up the prospects of a parish in Scotland to face the rigours of life in the backwoods settlements of the British colonies.

[1]Letter of MacGregor, McCulloch, and Ross, quoted in James Robertson, *History of the Mission of the Secession Church to Nova Scotia and Prince Edward Island* (Edinburgh, 1847), p. 240.

By the time the settlements were able to support a minister in anything like the manner to which he had been accustomed in Scotland, the settlements were dotted with congregations of Methodists; and Presbyterian people, weary of having their petitions for ministers ignored or disregarded, attached themselves to Methodist or Anglican congregations.

In the early period there were difficulties in adapting the Presbyterian tradition to conditions prevailing in frontier settlements. Rigid standards of ministerial training prevented the Presbyterian churches from obtaining a supply of ministers adequate to the needs of growing settlements. In situations that Methodists and Baptists were able to meet with lay-preachers and itinerant preachers, Presbyterians contented themselves with petitions to British presbyteries to send out more ministers. There was no inclination among the Canadian Presbyterian churches to adopt the procedure of the Cumberland Presbyterians in the United States in making ministerial standards more flexible to meet frontier conditions. Adherence to the parish system of church organization meant that Presbyterian churches could be maintained only in areas where there existed large groups of settlers from Scotland or the north of Ireland. Even where Presbyterian ministers made missionary tours in unchurched areas, their concern was not so much to make converts as to seek out Presbyterians.

The Secession ministers were more zealous than their Kirk brethren in responding to appeals to ministers in the frontier settlements, but all branches of Presbyterianism suffered losses in the beginning because of the difficulties of transferring the parish system of church administration to the colonial scene. William Proudfoot tells of organizing congregations and sending petitions for ministerial supply for them. When ministers could not be obtained, he says, "the people in many instances lost confidence." "Congregations dwindled away, and some made application to other denominations."[1] In the Maritimes, as Dr. Grant points out, many Presbyterians in New Brunswick and Prince Edward Island were "too widely scattered for efficient organization and adequate financial support." "Most of the settlers had become very careless about

[1]Unpublished letter of William Proudfoot to David Anderson, 1846.

religious observance by the time the first ministers reached them."[1]

Such causes as were established were situated in areas where the people had ties of ethnic homogeneity. In the Maritimes, "the great majority were Scots, whether from Scotland or northern Ireland. One group of Reformed immigrants from the continent held itself rather aloof; otherwise non-Scots had to consent to absorption." In the upper province William Proudfoot complained that the activity of the Secession churches had been limited largely to one racial group:

It has been a great hindrance to our success that we have kept up the Scotch character. We are too Scotch,—our habits, our brogue, our mode of sermonizing are all too Scotch. The thistle is everywhere seen; we have effected no lodgment in the public mind. . . . As at present constituted our mission is a foreign affair.[2]

He and others recognized that it would be necessary to train a native ministry before the church could really take root in colonial soil. In 1816 Thomas McCulloch had founded Pictou Academy "on the model of Presbyterian log colleges of the American frontier." "Soon, by the most informal methods, he was training ministers capable of competing with the graduates of Scottish universities." The programme of the church was strongly Scottish in tone:

The recalcitrance of the people was counteracted by a vigorous programme of Christian education and discipline. A rigorous examination at each communion season supplemented a constant catechesis from home to home. Preaching was exegetical, and Sunday Schools and Bible Classes were introduced at an early stage. . . .

Thanks largely to the exertions of a small group of missionaries, the Presbyterian churches of the Maritime Provinces were able to retain almost unimpaired the tradition imparted to them. In faith and practice Maritime Presbyterianism was practically a replica of the Scottish pattern. Ministers, whether imported or locally trained, stocked their libraries with Scottish books and journals. They continued to follow current Scottish developments in theology and churchmanship. They even were able to interest many of their congregations in them.[3]

[1]John Webster Grant, "The Presbyterian Tradition in the Maritimes," paper presented to Faith and Order Commission.
[2]William Proudfoot, *op. cit.*
[3]John Webster Grant, *op. cit.*

Even in the Maritimes, where the Scottish tradition was so prominent, there were modifications produced by the local situation in which the churches found themselves.

The democratically organized United Presbyterians, dissenters in Scotland, were, in the Maritimes, the dominant group; in the long run they were in effect to absorb the Kirk and the Free Church. . . .

The Seceders themselves thawed out somewhat in the New World. The antinomian edges of the Erskines were eroded by the benevolent evangelicalism of Chalmers, and in time even hints of Arminianism ceased to shock.[1]

In the upper provinces, possibly because of a stronger feeling of Canadian nationalism, the original Scottish tradition was considerably modified.

The Kirk in Upper and Lower Canada had fought a losing battle to obtain a favoured position, along with the Church of England, as a state-supported church. With the failure of its attempt to secure a favoured status it was forced to accept the voluntary method of support. Instead of being in a favoured position of dominance, as in Scotland, the Kirk found itself contending against the claims of the Church of England to be the established church, and competing with dissenting bodies, such as the Methodists, who were aggressively evangelical. In this situation the Kirk found that it had to adapt itself to a new situation if it hoped to survive at all. In the process some of the provincialism of Scottish Presbyterianism was eroded. An editorial in the *Canadian Presbyter* in 1857 pointed out that a colonial church had certain advantages. It need not seek to reproduce in a new land and a new situation every feature of the ecclesiastical organization of the church in the homeland. It was in a position to prove all things, and to hold fast only to what it judged to be good. A minister of the Kirk Synod, when arguing for the practice of private communion, pointed out that many modifications had already been made in the practice of the church in Canada.

At the Synod of 1862 a very great change was introduced into the directory for public worship, a change so great that I wonder that it was accomplished so easily and quietly. On that occasion we went a great step in advance of every Presbyterian Church in the

[1] *Ibid.*

Empire when we permitted any of our Congregations to introduce instrumental music into its public services of praise. I held with others at that time that the innovation was needful in the circumstances of our Church.[1]

He pointed out that the Canadian church had similarly departed from Scottish precedents in providing services at the burial of the dead:

It is a rule of our church . . . that at the burial of the dead no prayers shall be offered at the place of interment. The law works well enough in Scotland where it is universally observed. . . . But does the Law work well in the Colony? It works so ill that in many places it is utterly disregarded.[2]

His observation reflected the situation of the church in a new setting, a "mixed community" in which it was "hurtful for a single church to go in the teeth of the Christian sentiments of all others."

The situation of the Canadian Presbyterian churches fostered in them a greater sense of missionary responsibility than was found in Presbyterianism in Scotland. Professor A. L. Farris offers three explanations for this:

1. The Canadian churches were themselves the products of missionary activity, and it was natural that after having attained some measure of stability and security they should look to the needs of others.

2. In the old land missionary work tended to be done by the great missionary societies which were not organically related to the life of the church. Such societies were supported by contributions from wealthy patrons. In Canada the missionary thrust tended to be built more into the total structure of the church's mission.

3. The fact that Canada was such a large country, and that pioneering and homesteading continued for many generations, is of considerable significance. The existence of the frontier contributed to the fostering of the conviction that the church's concern must be with mission. There was a mission field continually confronting the church—the hinterland, the west and the north. This shaped the church's thinking, deployed her manpower, and determined her expenditures. The fact that such outreach had to be paid for by

[1]Letter of John Hay in the *Presbyterian*, November, 1867, p. 330.
[2]*Ibid.*

voluntary financing is significant, for it involved the average church member in the outreach of the church in two important ways: his interest had to be won through persuasive measures, and his interest tended to follow his contribution for outreach.[1]

Numerous factors contributed to the making of a Canadian outlook in the Presbyterian churches in Canada. All made efforts to train a native ministry. All made gallant efforts to issue periodicals that would give information concerning their work. All were aware of the necessity of interesting laymen in the work of the church and attempting to secure their support for its projects. Proximity to the United States involved all the churches, more or less, in a process of Americanization. While maintaining strong Scottish ties the Canadian church was influenced by the propaganda for the temperance movement in the United States, by the American Sunday School movement, and to some extent by American revivalism. The American churches, with greater resources in money and manpower, were able to experiment more freely than their Canadian brethren with new techniques of church work. Canadian churchmen frequently made use of the results of such experimentation or adapted the results for Canadian use. It is typical of their attitude that at the Pre-Assembly Congress of 1913, where stress was placed upon Canada's place among the family of nations, the members listened respectfully to an address from an American churchman on the subject, "How we raised a Million Dollars."[2] While anti-American and pro-British in political sentiment, Canadian churchmen, like Canadian citizens generally, have been receptive to many American influences. The resulting blend is neither American nor British, but Canadian.

III

American churchmen are sometimes impressed with the fact that Canadian Presbyterianism was able to achieve a national unity as early as 1875 while in the United States the process of unification is still going on. The difference is to be explained in part by differences in the political development of Canada and the United States, and

[1]A. L. Farris, in paper submitted to Faith and Order Commission, 1961.
[2]Address of A. E. Corey, Pre-Assembly Congress, 1913, pp. 321-327.

in part by differences of the situation in which Presbyterian churches have had to work.

In the United States national unity came earlier than in Canada. The American colonies were united from the beginning in a strong common loyalty. Regional differences between the North and South developed later, and national unity was only maintained through the long and costly struggle of the Civil War. In Canada we began with separate and isolated colonies which were united politically in 1867. While the American colonies turned their backs upon Europe to pursue their own course of national expansion, the colonies of British North America retained strong ties with the British Isles. The strength of nationalistic sentiment in the United States tended to make the American scene a melting pot in which European traditions were Americanized. When unity was achieved by the colonies of British North America it was unity which had to recognize the existence of, and permit the perpetuation of, diversities of culture. In Confederation, Canada deliberately turned her back on the philosophy of the melting pot. The Protestant denominations in Canada have always had to be aware of the solid phalanx of French Roman Catholicism in Quebec.

All these factors are reflected in the difference between the development of the churches in the United States and in Canada. When American Protestantism had about three hundred distinct religious groups, there were about seventy in Canada. Professor Keith Markell[1] points out that the following factors played a part in creating this difference.

1. Some of the American divisions were divisions between Negro and white churches. There was nothing parallel to this segregation of church groups in Canada.

2. Some of the divisions in the American churches came about through conflict over the issue of slavery and the Civil War. There were no such divisive issues to disturb the Canadian churches.

3. The strength of British ties with the Canadian colonies, and the preponderance of immigration from the British Isles in the early periods of development, meant that the churches that were strong in

[1]This and following references to statements by Professor Keith Markell are from a letter to Professor A. L. Farris, quoted in the paper presented by A. L. Farris.

the British Isles were strong in the colonies. "As late as 1915 Roman Catholics, Anglicans, Presbyterians and Methodists constituted eighty-five per cent of the Canadian Church population."

4. The formation of national religious bodies in Canada, following upon the achievement of political unity in 1867, was not followed by sectional rivalry as in the United States. "All of these factors," says Professor Markell, "help to account for the greater fragmentation in American Protestantism, without assuming that there has been some mysterious unitive force operating in Canada."

With this general background, common to all the major Protestant churches in Canada, it is easier to understand how the Presbyterian bodies in Canada were able to achieve their unity.

All branches of the family of Presbyterian churches at work in the provinces of British North America had much in common. All professed to accept the Westminster Confession of Faith as a subordinate standard of doctrine. All accepted the Westminster Directory for Public Worship as a guide for worship. All had a common form of church polity. The differences of theological opinion on questions concerning the relationships of church and state that had created most of the divisions in Scotland had little or no relevance in the Canadian situation. The unfortunate, and in many respects tragic, disruption of the British North American churches in the Free Church controversy was an unhappy consequence of the emotional involvement of some of the Canadian ministers in the affairs of the church in Scotland. At the meeting of the Canadian Synod in 1844 the members agreed unanimously that there was in Canada complete freedom in the election of ministers, that there was no interference from the state in the ecclesiastical courts, and that there was no prospect of such interference.[1] There was, however, a carry-over to the colonial churches of the heat generated in the Scottish controversy. The action of the Free Church of Scotland in sending out deputies to present their position and enlist support for their stand in the colonial churches helped to encourage the participation of the colonial churches in a

[1]Minutes, Synod of Presbyterian Church in Canada, 1844, p. 10. The division of the Canadian churches on this issue is considered in the author's essay, "By Schism Rent Asunder," *Canadian Journal of Theology*, Vol. 1, No. 3, pp. 175-183.

controversy that had no immediate relevance for them. The division in Presbyterian ranks brought about by this controversy lasted until the churches came together again in the union of 1875.

Practical considerations concerning the status of the Presbyterian churches in the colonies and concern for their survival amidst vigorous competition from other church groups were constant incentives encouraging the Presbyterian groups to strengthen their position by uniting their forces. The first union, between the Burgher and Anti-Burgher presbyteries in Nova Scotia, for instance, was brought about, in part at least, by the urgency of the necessity for supporting Pictou Academy. The union between the Kirk Synod and the United Synod in Upper Canada in 1840 was brought about by the urgency of being in a stronger position to claim a share in state support already being given to the Church of England. The union of 1875 followed in the wake of the political unity achieved in Confederation. Uniting bodies expressed the desire to have a strong, united Presbyterian Church to take its place in the shaping of the life of the new dominion.

The results achieved by the unions prior to 1875 did not always fulfil the expectations of those who laboured to achieve them. Alex F. Kemp, who had been a supporter of the union between the Free Church and the United Presbyterian Church in 1861, expressed disappointment in 1867 at the results of the union. He noted that in a period of four years prior to the union the separated bodies had shown a rate of increase in membership of twelve per cent per annum, whereas after the union the rate of increase was only five per cent per annum. There were similar declines of the rate of increase in the number of ministers and in contributions for the work of the church. He concluded:

The results of our Union, so far, may be teaching us by experience, that Union is not always strength, and that the half sometimes exceeds the whole. The conclusion may be forcing itself on us that the united Powers of two moral forces are not always equal to the sum of both in separation.[1]

[1]A. L. Kemp, "Union," in the *Presbyterian*, March, 1867, pp. 78-80.

The appeal of having a stronger denominational organization to meet a highly competitive situation was, however, always an important factor in encouraging union among the Presbyterian bodies.

It played some part, too, in the movement towards the formation of the United Church in 1925. Protestant churches in Canada felt that their divisions placed them in a position of disadvantage when compared to the strong position of Roman Catholicism in Canada. Dr. Chown of the Methodist Church spoke in 1922 of the necessity for Protestantism in Canada to speak with a united voice. If it cannot do so, he said, "the future is not only dark—it is dismal, distracting, and distressing."

If I may venture to prophesy I would say with all conviction that if the major churches of Protestantism cannot unite, the battle which is going on now so definitely for the religious control of our country will be lost within the next few years.[1]

His views were shared by many advocates of church union in the Presbyterian Church who hoped that the creation of one strong, united Protestant church in Canada would give it an advantage for religious political action similar to that enjoyed by the Church of Scotland.

The provincial exclusiveness and isolationism of Scottish Presbyterianism was eroded in the mingling of denominations in Canada and in the necessity for denominational co-operation in projects of common concern. In the diaries and journals and letters of the first missionaries there are frequent expressions of horror at the strength of popery in Canada, and frequent expressions of disdain for the activities of Methodists, Baptists and other sectarian groups. Some of the early session records contain references to members of the church being disciplined for attending religious meetings sponsored by other religious bodies. These prejudices were gradually broken down. Union Sunday Schools were established in many areas, where all Protestant children were taught together. Members of the divided branches of Protestantism were exposed to the same cultural

[1]Quoted in C. E. Silcox, *Church Union in Canada*, p. 207.

influences. They were educated in the same schools; they read the same books, newspapers and magazines. Idiosyncrasies were rubbed off, and angular points of difference were eroded by the ubiquitous pressures towards cultural conformity. The growth of movements in which denominations co-operated to do tasks together which they could not do as well singly contributed to the unitive tendency in Canadian Protestantism. The work of such organizations as the Bible Society, the Evangelical Alliance, and various missionary and benevolent activities drew support from the major denominations. Presbyterians co-operated heartily in such interdenominational undertakings. Members of all the historic denominations found that they had much in common with brethren of other churches. Some of these factors were operative in the United States as they were in Canada. Added to the factors of the smallness of Canada's population and the fear on the part of the Protestant churches of Roman Catholic domination, they happened to work more strongly in Canada towards the achievement of unity.

It may be noted finally, that the magnitude of the task confronting the Canadian churches was an impetus towards unification. As Professor Farris states:

A very large factor contributing to the union movement in Canada was the smallness of the church in the face of the gigantic task which confronted her. This sense of responsibility for the fulfilment of a mission in Canada, together with the growing feeling that excessive competition limited the possibility of fulfilling this mission, was a powerful factor in the thinking of the church. In short it was felt that it was economically and spiritually wasteful not to be together. This was carried over with strength into the propaganda materials of the Unionist party of the Presbyterian Church in Canada prior to 1925.[1]

It may be added that laymen were particularly aware of this factor. Theological distinctions and differences seemed in their eyes to be of small consequence in the presence of the great tasks confronting all the churches of Canada together. In the Pre-Assembly Congress of 1913, in which lay participation was strong, great emphasis was placed upon the magnitude of the church's task in ministering to the new Canadians and in taking a fair share of responsibility for foreign missionary enterprise.

[1]A. L. Farris, *op. cit.*

IV

In any study of the development of the Canadian churches one is aware of conflicting currents of thought, of paradoxes, anomalies and inconsistencies. The mingling of influences from the United States and the British Isles, the additions constantly being made to the ministry and membership of the Canadian churches by recruits from the British churches, and the gradual development of a national point of view in Canada have all contributed to the shaping of the Canadian churches.

In regard to the changes effected in the Presbyterian tradition through its transplantation to Canada, we may note the following factors as having been most decisive.

1. The recognition that within the Presbyterian family of churches existing divisions had little significance in Canada. Whether ministers came from the Secession churches of Scotland or northern Ireland, from the Church of Scotland, or from other Presbyterian churches of the British Isles or the United States, their services were welcomed. In worship, in doctrine and in most of the usages of church life, these Presbyterian groups were in general agreement. It was natural that having so much in common, and being divided only on issues which were largely irrelevant in Canada they should come together, as they did, and merge in a series of unions that culminated in the union of 1875 and the formation of the Presbyterian Church in Canada. While the same divisions of Presbyterianism existed in the United States, American churches were not exposed to the same pressures towards unification as were operative in Canada. In the United States a much larger population permitted the maintenance of more religious groups than could be maintained in the small, isolated and scattered settlements of British North America.

2. The development of a Canadian national sentiment which recognized that the church must adapt itself to its Canadian setting. When political unity was achieved in 1867, the Presbyterian churches which had long been established in the separated colonies were prepared to merge their forces to minister more effectively in a dominion which was to extend from sea to sea.

Presbyterianism in Canada claims to be in historic continuity with the Church of Scotland as reformed in 1560. It has sought to maintain a tradition which it has prized highly. But it has also endeavoured to be a Canadian church, and to meet its responsibilities as a church of Jesus Christ at work in Canada.

NOTE: I am indebted for some of these observations to an essay by Dr. John Webster Grant on "The Presbyterian Tradition in the Maritime Provinces," and to an essay by Professor A. L. Farris on the changes wrought in Presbyterianism through its transplantation to British North America. I have indicated in the text where direct use has been made of their materials. For the final form of this essay, for a few additional materials, and for conclusions which may sometimes be at variance with those of Dr. Grant and Professor Farris, I must assume full responsibility

N.G.S.

5

IS THERE A CANADIAN BAPTIST TRADITION?

STUART IVISON

The Baptist tradition, like all others that make up our Canadian stream of life, was imported from elsewhere. It first entered Canada from the United States, where it had already been modified after crossing the Atlantic from Britain. Later it came directly into Canada from Britain, but in forms that had undergone considerable development in Britain itself. One of these forms was Scottish, the other English. The Baptist body in Canada today still shows to the careful observer these three main strata, American, Scottish and English, however they may have been welded together by the pressure of forces peculiar to our Canadian environment.

The Baptist movement of modern times has been called one of the "end products" of the Reformation. Its first leaders came from the ranks of the Independents and Separatists of the latter part of the sixteenth and earlier part of the seventeenth centuries. The extent to which these leaders had been influenced by European Anabaptists is still uncertain. Some Baptist historians of a generation ago were unwilling to see any connection between the Baptists of the seventeenth century and the pre-Reformation sects on the continent. This position is not much held today. Study of the sixteenth century Anabaptists is still proceeding, and reveals significant similarities between many of their views and those of the Baptists who appeared in history a century later. Similarity of views, however, does not necessarily imply direct historical connection.

One of the ablest of the English Separatists was John Smyth, a Fellow of Christ's College, Cambridge, and former Chaplain of the city of Lincoln, who around 1606 withdrew from the Church of England to become pastor of a small Separatist congregation. During 1607 and 1608 he and a number of his supporters, along with many Independents, were obliged to leave England and found refuge in Holland. There, in Amsterdam where he settled, Smyth founded a church in which the requirement for membership was a declaration of personal faith accompanied by the baptism of the professed believer. After long consideration he had come to regard the church not as a parochial institution, to which people belonged by being born in the parish, but as a gathered community, a group of professed believers, a fellowship of converted people. Admission should be by consent of the congregation following profession of faith and submission to the ordinance of baptism as a sign of obedience to Christ.

Early Congregationalists, led by John Robinson, who was also a refugee in Holland, took much the same position regarding the nature of the church but stopped short of believer's baptism. The renowned satirist Joseph Hall (1574-1656), who was to become Bishop of Exeter in 1627 and then Bishop of Norwich in 1641, attacked both Smyth and Robinson for their separation from the Church of England. He complimented Smyth, however, for being at least consistent, chiding Robinson for not going all the way to the Baptist position if he did not intend to return to the Anglican Church.

Returning from exile late in 1611 or early in 1612, followers of Thomas Helwys, a lay supporter of Smyth, formed the first Baptist Church in Britain in Spitalfields, London. This church, and five others that sprang up in the next fifteen years, were Arminian in doctrine. They stressed religious freedom and tolerance, in line with the teaching of Helwys, who published the first demand in England for full religious liberty for all, including "heretics, Turks, Jews or whatsoever." Helwys was far ahead of his time in this respect and was imprisoned in Newgate, where he died.

From these early Arminian Baptists, with their belief in a general atonement, their lack of emphasis on credal statements and their indifference to the finer points of theology and church government, there grew up in Britain the very considerable body known as General Baptists. In North America their influence was continued by the Free Baptists. They practised believer's baptism, which was administered by pouring water on the forehead, but they did not always demand such baptism as a prerequisite to membership in the church. John Bunyan was their most distinguished representative in the later years of the seventeenth century.

In the 1630's Baptist churches of a different stamp began to appear in England. These were Calvinist in doctrine and drew largely from the Westminster Confession of the Presbyterians in their statements of faith. Believing in a particular atonement, they became known as Particular Baptists. They stressed the sovereign will of God in human affairs and were more careful regarding forms of church government than were the General Baptists. They adopted baptism by immersion as their rule, apparently after discussion with continental Anabaptist leaders.

The ideas of the Particular Baptists had more thrust than those of the General Baptists, causing them to become the dominant force in the Baptist movement in America, where the adjective "Regular" was used to describe them. Though the two types of Baptists held many things in common, especially their view of the church as a "gathered community" and their conviction that baptism should be administered to "none but believers only," the two traditions followed separate paths on both sides of the Atlantic for nearly two centuries. In Britain the General Baptists produced a small group of extremists who eventually embraced the Unitarian position, while the Particular Baptists lost a minority who called themselves Strict Baptists. These secessions paved the way for the union of the majorities in both bodies, and the Baptist Union of Great Britain and Ireland was formed in 1891. It superseded a much less inclusive Baptist Union which had existed from as far back as 1813.

It is important to recognize that in Baptist life today, in Canada as elsewhere, these two strains of emphasis are still observable. The line that runs back through Free Baptists to their Anabaptist and Arminian origins has not been altogether obliterated, but it is intertwined with that which follows the Regular, Calvinist, Particular tradition, and in our Canadian churches the latter is the stronger of the two.

The first Baptist church in America was formed by Roger Williams at Providence, Rhode Island, in 1639. Persecuted by New England Puritans because he did not accept their ideas of a theocratic state, and ultimately banished from Massachusetts in 1635, Williams established the principle of religious liberty in the new colony which he founded in Rhode Island. For the next century the growth of the Baptist movement in the American colonies was slow, although by 1700 there were churches in Massachusetts, New Jersey, New York City, Long Island and Pennsylvania. In 1775 there were still less than ten thousand Baptists in America, of whom nearly half were in New England, the territory now occupied by the states of Maine, New Hampshire, Vermont, Massachusetts, Connecticut and Rhode Island.

With the coming of independence to the United States, and with the effects of the Great Awakening being felt throughout the whole American community, a period of phenomenal growth began for the Baptist denomination. Many factors contributed to this rapid increase, which between 1775 and 1800 raised the proportion of Baptists in the general population from one in 264 to one in 53, and by 1850 to one in 29. Discernible among such factors were:

1. The rise and increasing popularity of democratic ideas in the political realm. Baptists probably expressed the democratic ideal within the church more than any other body. This made their message acceptable where once it had been suppressed.

2. Since, according to some authorities, about ninety per cent of the population in the United States were outside of the Christian church altogether in the earlier part of the eighteenth century, a vast field for evangelism existed within the society where Baptists suddenly found themselves popular. Roused by the influence of the Great Awakening, they took advantage of this opportunity to gain thousands of adherents from among these previously un-churched people. At the same time, people who were influenced by the change in religious climate to seek church affiliation turned to the church that had been made popular by the trend of events.

3. In the pioneer communities on the frontier, Baptist church organization was sufficiently flexible to meet the local need. S. D. Clark has discussed this fully in his book *Church and Sect in Canada* (Toronto, 1948).

From 1760 onwards immigration from New England flowed into Nova Scotia, especially to its western part. Most of these settlers were of Puritan Congregationalist stock. They feared the Roman Catholic Church, which had been one of the instruments of French colonial expansion, and they had approved the removal of the French settlers in 1755. Their dislike of the Church of England was also pronounced. When, in turn, it became the ally of the official regime in Nova Scotia, they resisted its claims.

Yet, as S. D. Clark has shown, there were very severe stresses within the Congregationalist system. The Great Awakening from 1742 onwards in New England divided them into two factions, the extremely revivalist Newlights and the more conservative Oldlights. It was the Newlight element that produced in Nova Scotia the great revival that began in earnest in 1776 and continued on into the nineteenth century. The chief evangelist of this revival was Henry Alline (1748-1784), who after an intense experience of conversion and an equally strong sense of a call to preach, became a tremendous power among the settlers. Alline's refusal to wait for formal training before taking up his career antagonized the more conservative elements in Congregationalism. The effect of his preaching on Congregationalist churches was frequently disruptive. In place after place the Newlight elements that followed him broke away and formed themselves into separate congregations. Lacking pastoral oversight, many of them turned to their Baptist neighbours for fellowship, and ultimately became Baptist churches. Alline himself never became a Baptist, but he was much at home among them, where his revivalist preaching was warmly welcomed. Thus the force of the revival lent great momentum to the Baptist movement in the Maritimes. At the present time half of the population in some areas is reported in the census as Baptist.

The Baptist fellowship similarly provided a spiritual home, in at least one notable instance, for a group of Anglicans in search of a greater measure of control over their own church affairs. In 1827 some of the most prominent members of St. Paul's Anglican Church in Halifax withdrew to form the Granville Street Baptist Church. Some of these were very influential citizens and brought to the Baptist cause a distinct acquisition of educated leadership. From them came the impetus that resulted in the founding of Acadia University.

Baptist work in Ontario and Quebec was begun by the few Loyalists of that persuasion who entered the country during the American Revolution or shortly afterwards. They established liaison with Baptist missionary societies in New York and Boston, so that from 1802 until the War of 1812 there was a constant coming and going of itinerant missionaries across the border. Most of the churches founded by these leaders were of the Calvinist "Regular" type, though Free Baptist influence was in evidence in Ontario around Woodstock. Great emphasis was laid on each church being recognized by an "association," the Baptist counterpart of the presbytery, and without exception the churches in both Upper and Lower Canada belonged to such an association, either in Canada or the United States. During the war communication between Canadian Baptist churches and their sponsoring bodies across the border virtually ceased, but was resumed soon afterwards. Discussions regarding the desirability of keeping up this inter- national relationship took place with the result that by 1819 all "associational" ties with the United States had come to an end by mutual consent and the Canadian churches had formed associations of their own.

Immigration from Scotland into the Ottawa Valley from 1815 onwards brought a new type of Baptist influence into this part of Canada. Baptists have never been very numerous in Scotland, though officers and men of Cromwell's army helped to establish congregations there in the seventeenth century. In the latter part of the eighteenth century the Haldane brothers, Robert and James, conducted great evangelistic campaigns, establishing some thirty churches in Perthshire and a large church, with a training school for preachers, in Edinburgh. The Baptist churches in Montreal and Ottawa and along the Ottawa River owed their origin to this source.

The move to establish a Baptist college in this part of Canada was made by leaders of these Scottish immigrants, notably John Edwards of Clarence, near Ottawa, and John Gilmour of Montreal. It was in Montreal that the college was opened in 1838. Its teaching staff and financial support came mostly from England, where the Canada Baptist Missionary Society was formed to raise funds. The Canadian branch of the Society was directly responsible for the college but was not able to carry the load, and the college closed in 1849. Later, when the educational interests of the Baptists in Ontario and Quebec were transferred to western Ontario, more support was forthcoming. The Canadian Literary Institute was opened in Woodstock, Ontario, in 1860 with a theological department for the training of ministers and general academic courses up to the second year in arts of the University of Toronto. In 1881 Toronto Baptist College came into being to provide theological education, and the name of the Literary Institute was changed to Woodstock College. In 1887 a university charter was obtained, and through the generosity of Senator William McMaster the two colleges were combined to form McMaster University. This university, which moved to Hamilton, Ontario, in 1930, is now non-sectarian, but McMaster Divinity College, in affiliation with it, remains under Baptist control.

Other strands of influence from abroad entered Canadian Baptist life in the nineteenth century. In 1837 a small group of French Protestants from Switzerland took up residence near the Richelieu River between Montreal and the American border. There they established a French-speaking Baptist congregation and a residential school, known as Feller College after its founder, Madame Henrietta Feller. From this centre has grown a small group of French or bilingual Baptist churches, located all the way from Ottawa to Quebec City. In Nova Scotia, and in southwestern Ontario along the Detroit River, fugitive slaves established Baptist churches that have since grown to include some twenty thousand Negroes among their members and adherents. The earliest Baptist church in Toronto was one of these.

West of the Great Lakes, Baptists entered Manitoba in 1873 from Ontario, and a church was founded in Winnipeg in 1875. As settlers moved out to the prairies, Baptist missionaries went with them. British Columbia's first Baptists came from the state of Washington, but the churches of that province, like those of Manitoba, Saskatchewan and Alberta, are part of the Baptist Union of Western Canada.

Twentieth-century immigration from Europe has brought groups of Baptists from many countries, including Scandinavia, Poland, Russia and the Ukraine, Hungary and Germany. Swedes, Norwegians and Germans have their own conferences to which their churches belong, and these include as many or more churches in the United States as in Canada. One German conference, known in the United States as "North American Baptists," has recently become incorporated in this country as "North American Baptists of Canada." In these northern European language groups, ethnic ties are very strong, and church organization is used as a means to

preserve cultural identity. It is important to remember that the
Baptist movement in Europe in modern times was not indigenous
but is the result of contacts by Europeans with the Baptists of
Britain and the United States in the nineteenth and twentieth
centuries.

Have these various forms of the Baptist tradition from abroad
combined in this country to form a distinctive Canadian Baptist
tradition? This question is related to the larger one, "What is
Canadianism?"

"No one knows my country," wrote Bruce Hutchison, "neither
the stranger nor its own sons. My country is hidden in the dark and
teeming brain of youth upon the eve of manhood. My country has
not found itself nor felt its power nor learned its true place."
Elsewhere the same writer has described Canadians as being
apologetic, pitifully inarticulate, singularly lacking in humour,
unable to laugh at themselves. "Maybe," he says, "we think our
poetry and laughter are inferior to other people's, and so repress
them." He concludes that "our main characteristic is just this
refusal to construct a national character. . . . We have taken a
nothing, a pathological horror of expression, and erected a something which distinguishes us from all other people."

Another contemporary Canadian writer, Lister Sinclair, in search
of the elusive "Canadian idiom" in literature, wonders whether it
is not just a matter of applying British syntax to an American
vocabulary. He too finds that we are reluctant to give full expression
to our thoughts and feelings. He cannot account for this "calculated
diffidence," and speculates that it must come from the soil because
it seems to engulf even newcomers to our land. He concludes, however, that if our literature has a characteristic note, it can best be
described as "irony." Malcolm Ross, the essayist and critic, agrees
with this, and says bluntly, "Irony is the key to our identity."

However difficult it may be to identify the typical Canadian
Baptist, it is not difficult to see at least some of the ways in which
the combined traditions of our communion in Canada have been
modified by social, political and geographical influences. Geography
and politics combined in the eighteenth and early nineteenth centuries
to determine the migration routes that brought Baptists into Canada.
Once here, geography made it difficult for Baptists in different parts

of Canada to get in touch with each other. After several abortive attempts to achieve some form of all-Canadian Baptist unity, the Baptist Federation of Canada was formed in 1944. The chief architect of the federation, in its final stages, has written that it came into being because the committee set up by the three regional Baptist bodies "hit upon the federal principle." The truth is that it is a federation of the loosest possible kind and has not yet become a means of expressing the common aims of Canadian Baptists. Its framers seemed unable to see any middle way between such a loose federation and what they fearfully described as "proposals of monolithic unity," though it has never been established that any such proposals were ever made.

In a sense, the conflicts of jurisdictions in federal and provincial politics are reflected within the Baptist organization, except that the latter is still a long way from reaching even the limited though very real unity achieved by the provinces in 1867. The federal government can speak for Canada as a whole in international affairs, and can negotiate treaties and trade agreements with other nations. Within the broad range of its authority it can move freely, being answerable to the electorate through Parliament. The Baptist Federation, on the other hand, has not yet assumed any major role in Canadian Baptist life. Its triennial assembly is a fraternal gathering that hears reports of committees but deals with none of the major enterprises of the Baptist denomination. It plays little or no part in framing policy with regard to overseas missions, education or publication. It has been unable to apply for membership in the World Council of Churches because two of its constituent bodies have not yet approved this step and show no sign of doing so.

The Canadian Baptist tradition has, like other church traditions in Canada, been affected by the impact of modern biblical scholarship. The withdrawal of the great London preacher C. H. Spurgeon from the Baptist Union of Great Britain in 1887 was caused by the controversy then going on in most Protestant bodies in Britain and Europe. Evangelicals in all churches were alarmed at the radical views of scriptural revelation that were being propounded as a result of applying the techniques of literary and historical criticism to the Bible. Though the main stream of Baptist tradition has been against formal creeds and has emphasized the liberty of the individual

Christian to exercise his private judgment in interpreting the Scriptures, some Baptists, in their anxiety to preserve evangelical doctrines, turned to credal statements as a means of defining their position. Spurgeon himself regarded as satisfactory the doctrinal statement of the Evangelical Alliance, an interdenominational body that promoted, among other things, the Universal Week of Prayer. Disbanding the "College Conference," a ministerial group consisting mostly of pastors trained in his own college, he reorganized it on a credal basis to make sure that its members were doctrinally sound. Even then, he was forced to make some exceptions for the sake of men who were undoubtedly conservative in their views but objected to subscribing to any formal creed as a test.

There were not a few in Britain who feared that Spurgeon's withdrawal from the Union would utterly wreck the Baptist denomination in that country. His international fame as a preacher and his immense prestige among his co-religionists made him for many years the leading Baptist in the world. Nevertheless, the Union proved to be more representative of the distinctive elements in the Baptist tradition than the great individual who withdrew from it. Neither his personal genius nor his world-wide influence could outweigh the Baptist instinct for liberty to interpret and freedom to apply the truths of the Bible according to the light of progress. The attempt to harden the Baptist tradition into a rigid pattern failed, and those who were willing to entrust that tradition to the future unencumbered by credal limitations were proved, on the whole, to represent the Baptist mind.

The unrest occasioned by the controversy over biblical criticism was evident to some degree among Canadian Baptists by 1910, but it did not reach its peak until the 1920's. The storm centre was in the city of Toronto, where the brilliant and eloquent minister of Jarvis Street Baptist Church, T. T. Shields, became the leader of the fundamentalist wing. His attack was directed chiefly against the theological faculty of McMaster University, but he did not hesitate to single out ministers in other parts of the country as targets for his criticism. American fundamentalists, some Baptist and some of other denominations, were frequently invited to the Jarvis Street pulpit to lend support to the Canadian campaign. As time went on, it was more and more evident that historic Baptist principles were not really at stake. The controversy was a local reflection of a wide-spread fundamentalist movement that cut across all denominational boundaries and appeared in one way or another in all Protestant church bodies.

Jarvis Street Church was expelled from the Baptist Convention of Ontario and Quebec, however, because it and several other churches had formed a rival organization to which they sought to divert support from the missionary agencies of the Convention. On their expulsion, the dissident churches and ministers were joined by others until about one-fifth of the churches had broken away from the main body. These had difficulty in finding a common ground of unity, and for nearly thirty years were organized as two separate groups, known as The Union of Regular Baptist Churches and The Fellowship of Independent Baptist Churches. Both of these fundamentalist bodies found their main support in Ontario, though a number of churches in other provinces joined one or other of them. In 1955 they united to form "The Fellowship of Evangelical Baptist Churches," and subsequently they were incorporated by Act of Parliament under that name.

The Evangelical Baptist Churches are now attempting to parallel the historic Baptist form of church organization by setting up local associations. The task is not easy. Half of their churches, having belonged for many years to a body dominated by one personality, are unused to democratic procedures. The "Independent" churches were fearful of any and all "associational" ties, and it is to be doubted whether they have yet grasped the significance of the association as it was conceived by the Baptists who first adopted it in the seventeenth century. If they fail to do so, they are unlikely to make it an effective instrument of Baptist policy. In addition, they are proceeding in the opposite direction to the historic development. The early associations took form as a logical outgrowth of church life in answer to a specific need. They preceded, rather than followed, larger groupings, whereas in the case of the present-day Evangelical Baptists, incorporation as a national body came first and the move to form associations is coming later. In a reversal of the historical process, associations are being fitted into a pre-determined framework.

It is questionable whether the fundamentalist variant of the Canadian Baptist tradition has really modified it to any significant degree. As in Britain, the main body of Baptists had no objection to biblical literalism on the part of individuals who preferred that point of view. Tension arose when those who belonged to the literalist school sought to impose a credal formula on the whole denomination as the price of their support of missionary endeavour. Baptists had to maintain the right of private judgment in the face of this challenge if they were to continue as the bearers of a living tradition. They accepted the fundamentalist challenge at great cost in numerical strength, but they maintained their historic principle.

Not all of those who took the fundamentalist side in the disruption were ready to subscribe to a formal creed. Still fewer were ready to accept the undisputed leadership of the American fundamentalist orators who crossed the border at frequent intervals to instruct Canadian opinion. There was something about these persuaders, powerful though they were, that did not attract the theological conservatives among Canadian Baptists. Some of the seceders found their way back into the main body as the years passed, to enjoy once more the fellowship of a tradition they had never ceased to love but which for a time they had misunderstood. After a while, also, the seceding churches ceased on the whole to look across the border for their inspiration. Their Canadianism has proved too strong to allow them to be absorbed into an American fundamentalist amalgam, in which the Baptist tradition as such is only incidental.

One effect of the controversy on the main body has been to discourage free, uninhibited utterance on the part of their most gifted ministers. Baptist assemblies seldom hear truly prophetic preaching these days. No Baptist publication in Canada at the present time provides a forum for the exchange of adventurous ideas. Those who speak in public or write for Canadian Baptist journals are for the most part careful to follow the accepted line and to promote the official programme. There are, undoubtedly, prophetic spirits amongst us, but their voices speak only from their own pulpits, and to people who know them well enough to understand them. Remembering still the distorted versions of sincere expression that were spread abroad in days of controversy, and the frustration of trying to be understood, sensitive men have been driven in upon themselves. To the observer, it would appear that the robust quality of the tradition has to some extent departed.

Or is this apparent diffidence but an aspect of the Canadian character showing itself in religious life as it does in literature and the arts? Are we passing from the over-confidence of immaturity through a period of self-questioning to a stronger, more mature outlook? As the national character casts off its dependence upon direct ties with older cultures, ceases to imitate them, and assumes its own status, it is reasonable to expect that church traditions will do the same. We cannot escape the influence of the past, and the roots of our present life as a people lie deep in many countries. England, Scotland and the United States have provided the greater part of our heritage, and their hold upon us is still powerful. Indeed, the influence of the United States on our religious life and institutions, as upon all other aspects of our Canadian culture, is hardly relaxed for a single hour each day.

Nevertheless, there has been and still is a determination on the part of Canadian Baptists to work out their problems within their own household, and to do so as Canadians. In this way they reflect the attitude of Canadian political leaders, who since the winning of responsible government have been trying to fashion in this part of the continent a home that Canadians can call their own. Alexander Mackenzie, second prime minister after Confederation, was a Baptist who had emigrated from Scotland in 1842 as a youth in his twenties. Throughout his public career, and especially during his term of office from 1873 to 1878, he opposed American aggressiveness on the one hand and the excessive claims of British imperialists on the other. He cherished the dream, shared by thousands, though they were not always able to express it, of a national community, free and independent, gradually taking shape on the great northern land mass between the two oceans. The passion to play a part in the building of such a community is perhaps a more accurate key to Canadian identity than the "irony" described by our literary representatives.

The Canadian Baptist community, except in Nova Scotia, has not so far experienced any period of growth comparable to that which took place in the United States between 1775 and 1850. At no time in Canadian history has there been a combination of religious, political and social factors to provide them with such an opportunity. From the arrival of the first settlers until now, the vast majority of the people have already had some acknowledged church affiliation. There has been no great vacuum created by a massive breaking away from the historic churches such as characterized American society in the period culminating in the rationalism of Jefferson and Paine. Hence there has been no occasion for such a wholesale return to church affiliation as was brought about after that period in the United States was over.

Even by 1850, according to the 1962 issue of the *Yearbook of American Churches*, only sixteen per cent of the people of the United States were members of any church or synagogue. The remaining eighty-four per cent provided a vast field for evangelism of which Baptists took advantage. By 1900, total church and synagogue membership still represented only thirty-six per cent of the population, whereas in Canada at that date four major denominations— Roman Catholic, Methodist, Presbyterian and Anglican—accounted for eighty-five per cent of the whole population.

In Britain also, it may be noted, the period in which Baptists increased most rapidly was that following the Evangelical Revival, when Nonconformity in general produced a galaxy 'of great preachers. With the passing of deism and the return of religious interest, the rising new middle class provided the main strength of the Nonconformist denominations. At the same time, the social concern generated by the revival enabled the Nonconformists to maintain contact with the new working class created by the Industrial Revolution. By the end of the nineteenth century this trend had passed its zenith, and the beginning of a period of consolidation was reflected by the formation of the Baptist Union of Great Britain and Ireland.

In a society as stable and conservative as that of Canada, people do not readily change their religious affiliations. When they do so, they tend to move towards churches that have accommodated them-selves to the *mores* of the community at large. Religious groups whose doctrines and practices sharply differentiate them may produce outstanding individuals, but they are unlikely to increase in members as rapidly as others. It has been difficult for Baptists in Canada to gain widespread acceptance for their doctrine of the church as a "gathered community," in which each individual must profess personal faith before being admitted.

Churches in which the first steps towards membership are taken by proxy during infancy seem to be preferred by most Canadians. Subsequent confirmation is less demanding and not nearly as lonely a decision as that required of those who wish to acquire full membership in a Baptist church. To receive Christian baptism after reaching the years of full self-consciousness, and in the intensely dramatic form of immersion, demands deep personal conviction and, in many instances, real moral courage. Children of Baptist parents, though prepared by family tradition and example for this mode of initiation into the church, are nevertheless not spared the necessity of individual choice. Many of them find it easier to affiliate with a church of the parochial type than to identify themselves with the more exclusive "gathered" church. Most people in Canada have been reared in traditions that made them members of a national church through being born into a certain nation as citizens, or members of a parochial church by being born into a family of that religious persuasion. Though there is no national church in Canada, the churches in this country which are of the parochial type are nearly all offshoots of national churches in other countries. Only a small minority of immigrants bring with them a tradition of the "gathered" church. Ours is a task of continually breaking new ground. Yet it is a task that must be done if the New Testament doctrine of the church is to be adequately interpreted. The church of the future will be deficient if the concept of the "gathered community" is neglected or forgotten, and—more serious still—the gospel will not be fully preached.

The phenomenal growth of the Baptist communion in the southern United States in recent times attracts the attention of their Canadian brethren and leads some to suggest that their methods and forms of organization might have similar results here. Yet Canadian Baptists going to live in the southern states are more likely to attend the Presbyterian church than the Baptist, and when representatives of the Southern Baptists come amongst us they seldom display any unusual talent or have any novel contribution to make to our church life. It appears that in the south, as in some other areas, the pattern of society in general has presented a need which Baptists of the Southern type have been able to meet to a considerable extent in the past, but that new social patterns already in evidence may make demands that will require very radical changes in Baptist forms of expression there.

For the first time in a century or more, membership gains in churches and synagogues of the United States show signs of levelling off. Since 1945 such gains had more than kept pace with the population increase, but in 1960 they were just about in proportion to the natural growth of the nation. As they enter a period of consolidation rather than expansion, the churches south of the border will, like those in Britain and Canada, be compelled to study with great care the structure of the society in which they work, and the resources at their disposal. They will still have much to teach us that will be of value, but it would be a mistake to assume that by imitating them we can best communicate the message of the gospel to our Canadian people. The two nations have much in common, but they are not the same.

The determination of Canadian Baptists to be themselves, while co-operating with their co-religionists through the world-wide fellowship of the Baptist World Alliance may, after all, be wisdom of a superior kind. In any case, it seems to reflect the present mood of Canadians in general. We owe too much to other traditions to do much boasting about our own—just yet. We do not propose to throw away anything of real value that has come to us from Britain or the United States or Europe. But neither do we propose to accept for ourselves a ready-made image of what we ought to be, whether inherited from one of the traditions that have gone into our making or invented by those who feel that they know what is best for us. If, as John Robinson said, "the Lord [hath] more light and truth yet to breake forth out of his holy Word," it seems likely that those who in the meantime do their work patiently and are true to themselves will not be denied that light and truth when they do break forth.

6

THE PEOPLE CALLED METHODISTS IN CANADA

GOLDWIN FRENCH

The Methodist Church that was absorbed into The United Church of Canada in 1925 was and had long been one of the largest Protestant denominations in this country. Its history went back to the distant era of pre-Loyalist Nova Scotia; its important place in Canadian life was a perennial object of comment and, to the Methodists themselves, a source of satisfaction. An understanding of the Methodist tradition is thus of great importance in comprehending the subsequent development of the United Church and other aspects of the religious history of Canada.

Recently one theologian wrote: "The tradition of a particular church is an extremely complex entity which involves a certain forming of the Christian mind, often in its subconscious depths. This 'mind' manifests itself in a definite way of 'seeing' and speaking as well as in typical identifying signs and reaction patterns."[1] What, then, was the shape of the Canadian Methodist "mind," especially as contrasted with the "minds" of other Methodist bodies? Further, what elements in the Methodist outlook facilitated or hindered its identification with other Protestant churches and with the Christian tradition as a whole?

I

Although it is manifestly impossible here to analyse the entire history of Canadian Methodism, the Methodist way of "seeing and speaking" can scarcely be understood without reference to several aspects of that history. Among these the most important were the teaching and practice of John Wesley and the forces to which the Methodist societies were exposed during their first half-century of growth.

[1]G. W. H. Lampe and D. M. Paton, eds., *The Old and the New in the Church* (London: S. C. M. Press, 1961), p. 15.

When Wesley, that true but unrecognized son of the eighteenth century, was asked to describe a Methodist, he replied: "A Methodist is one who has 'the love of God shed abroad in his heart by the Holy Ghost . . . ;' one who 'loves the Lord his God with all his heart and with all his soul, and with all his mind, and with all his strength.' . . ."[1] In other words, a Methodist was simply a Christian. In reality Methodism was a more complex entity than Wesley admitted or than its enemies realized.

Whatever may be said about the nature and validity of Wesley's religious insights, he was in his own eyes an orthodox Anglican who felt that he had a special mission to share those insights, especially with those who were not being reached by the church in his generation. The essence of his conviction was that corrupt men cannot contribute to their own salvation; rather, each man is set upon the Christian path by the direct intervention of the Holy Spirit. Moreover, he was firmly convinced that divine grace is available to all who humbly seek it and that those who receive it will have a living assurance of the presence of God in their hearts. But Wesley was equally sure that justification must be followed by sanctification in this life. Christian perfection, or holiness—the phrases he preferred—could be attained only by sincere and energetic participation in the spiritual and moral life of the Christian community, and finally by a second definitive act of the Holy Spirit. It was this doctrine of holiness that Wesley conceived it to be his duty to preach; he sought converts in order that they might be enabled to proceed towards the end of perfection.

This teaching, in conjunction with certain features of Wesley's personality and of the social circumstances of those who heeded his words, produced a religious community with some distinctive characteristics. The Methodist societies or church consisted of converts whose services were simple and fervently evangelical. They met regularly in small groups or classes in which faults were confessed and mutual admonitions were issued. They were much given to private worship and preserved a reverent attitude towards the sacraments. As individuals who sought to attain perfection they had a dynamic concern for the welfare of others, but they were

[1] John Wesley, *The Works of the Reverend John Wesley, A.M.*, ed. T. Jackson (3rd ed., London, 1829), VIII, 341.

deterred from political action by Wesley's conservative views. They were not greatly interested in their relationship with the wider tradition of the church, and, in keeping with Wesley's own pragmatic approach, they were oblivious of the doctrinal and practical difficulties posed by his beliefs. In short, whatever Wesley's intentions, they felt that theirs was the true and uncomplicated way to eternal life.

The organization of the Methodist Church was in keeping with its functions and with Wesley's position. The societies were grouped in circuits, each staffed by one or more itinerant preachers selected and trained by Wesley. The itinerants were assisted by local preachers and class leaders picked by Wesley or by themselves. The whole church was supervised by the annual conference of ministers, which met under Wesley's chairmanship and was, while he lived, the vehicle of his autocratic will. The entire system was flexible and efficient, but it had elements of tension in Wesley's legacy of imperious control and in the large role that it assigned to laymen.

From the start, indeed, the faith and the polity of Methodism were poised uneasily between possible extremes. The Methodist societies could become more evangelical or more intent upon the devoted practice of the Christian life. They could retire from the world or play a broadening part in its affairs. Deprived of Wesley's Anglican background, Methodism was likely to succumb to theological weakness or subversion, whereas in different social circumstances it might find itself without an audience. Similarly, its system of government might develop along autocratic and hierarchical lines or might become increasingly democratic and lay-centred. The manner in which these potentialities were exploited in a new environment shaped the Methodist "mind" in Canada.

II

Naturally these considerations were far from the minds of those simple people who began to expound Methodist ideas in Nova Scotia in 1779 and in the future province of Ontario in Upper Canada several years later. Their success was sufficiently great to attract the attention of the Methodist Episcopal Church of America. Organized in 1784, this church assumed control of the work in Nova

Scotia in that same year and subsequently took charge of that in Upper Canada. This latter association was maintained until 1828, but in 1800 the preachers in the eastern provinces transferred their allegiance to the English Wesleyan conference.[1]

These events, occurring early in the history of Canadian Methodism, had important consequences for its subsequent development. The Methodists in the Maritime Provinces did not secure effective autonomy from the English Conference until the creation of the Conference of Eastern British America in 1855. The restraining and conservative influence of the Wesleyans, together with the regular dispatch of missionaries from England, retarded the emergence of an independent outlook in the Maritime societies and the adaptation of their techniques to local needs. On the other hand, the size, the poverty and the geography of these provinces made it exceptionally difficult for them to reach their people. Methodist teaching itself had a rather limited appeal in an area containing heavy concentrations of Presbyterians and having a native evangelical tradition— the Newlight-Baptist—that was more acceptable to many. The one Methodist asset, the relative favour in which they were held by the influential people of this region, was of limited value in that it made unnecessary serious consideration of the Methodist place in this society.

In this new situation there emerged a distinctive type of Methodism that would become in time a part of the larger Canadian Methodist body. It was one in which there was impressive fidelity to Wesley's purposes, but in which his ends were sought rather more decorously than by his followers in the United States and Upper Canada. The preachers were reluctant to introduce popular devices for the ingathering of souls such as the camp meeting; in contrast many of them favoured the use of gowns and Wesley's liturgy, outward symbols of an inner urge towards a settled religious life. Although they preached the doctrine of "holiness," seemingly they were more interested in its moral than in its evangelical aspects. They were content, too, to believe that Methodism was the best form of Christianity and supposed that all right-thinking people would recognize the fact.

[1]These and subsequent statements on the early history of Canadian Methodism are documented in the writer's *Parsons and Politics* (Toronto: Ryerson, 1962).

In organization, there was no significant departure from the Wesleyan pattern. Until the formation of the conference the district meetings functioned, as in England, as local supervisory agencies and as vehicles of the Wesleyan Conference's policy. Distance, however, transformed the district meetings into miniature conferences not always willing to carry out decisions made in England. Moreover, the missionaries did not have the same antipathy to lay interests as did the English conference. Hence, when the Conference of Eastern British America was formed, its members were ready to assume new responsibilities and to consider possible structural changes.

Similarly, the attitude of these Methodists towards secular issues reflected the blend of local and external pressures to which they were long subjected. They were very proud of their deserved reputation for loyalty to the imperial connection, but they were also conscious of their colonial identity and acquired from the parent conference itself a nationalist and imperialist impulse. They emulated the latter in their contempt for party politics, their apparent fondness for conservative groups and their willingness to defend their own interest by political manoeuvres. Their chief secular interest was education, but even in this case it was their own need of trained preachers rather than the general needs of the community that led them to act. In relation to society, indeed the Maritime Methodist tradition was generally one of narrowness and hesitancy, but it was susceptible to development on broader lines.

III

In contrast, the peculiar combination of circumstances that shaped the rise of Methodism in Upper Canada imparted a different quality to the Methodist "mind" in that province. From the Methodist Episcopal Church, to which Upper Canadian Methodists belonged until 1828, came a variety of preachers and administrators whose deficiencies in education were more than offset by their zeal and self-sacrifice. Their teaching was in keeping with Wesley's convictions, but inevitably it was not identical with them. These men had no lingering affection for the Church of England; rather they belonged to a new church whose primary task was the rescue of all those souls who stood near the gates of hell. They used the class meeting and took pains to curb the immoral behaviour of their people, but they emphasized strongly that sanctification was to be gained by the "second blessing," another emotional conversion experience. Consequently their conduct of worship and their preaching were marked invariably by impassioned appeals to the emotions, the consciences and often the fears of their auditors. Inevitably excesses occurred, but it would be wrong to suppose that exuberant manifestations were the substance of the religious lives of most Methodists. Rather these early preachers created a body of converts who genuinely sought perfection in a tense and dynamic spiritual atmosphere.

Secondly, both preachers and people shared in a system of church government that departed considerably from the original Wesleyan polity. Its quadrennial general or legislative conferences and its regional annual conferences for administrative purposes gave it a high degree of adaptability and flexibility. The representative general conference was the supreme legislative body in the Methodist church. It had to work within constitutional limits, however, for its authority was balanced by an itinerant episcopate and the district presiding eldership. Above all, the bishops and the conference maintained the circuit itinerancy. All preachers had to range as widely as possible, and they were moved regularly from circuit to circuit so that their talents might be employed most effectively. Yet, vigorously as conferences and bishops wielded their authority, they also promoted the circuit quarterly meeting, not only as a religious agency but as a means of maintaining a close relationship between clerical and lay interests.

In Upper Canada, as in the United States, the Methodist Episcopal preachers were remarkably successful in building up a growing body of adherents. In so doing, however, they raised a potential native leadership and stimulated the development of an independent outlook among their converts. After 1815 these Canadian societies and their preachers became increasingly conscious of the hostility roused by their American affiliation. As the tide of local political controversy rose, they grew determined to acquire independent status, a wish that was reluctantly granted by the American General Conference in 1828.

The Methodist Episcopal Church of Upper Canada was in doctrine and organization similar to its parent. The episcopate quickly became moribund, however, whereas the authority of the quarterly meetings was strengthened slightly at the expense of the conference. Even more striking was the vigour with which this church engaged in political controversy. Faced with what it considered to be a threat to its own interests and to the well-being of Upper Canada, it championed the separation of church and state, the recognition of the constitutional rights of Upper Canadians and the establishment of a comprehensive and popular system of primary and secondary education. In so doing it acquired a somewhat exaggerated reputation for political and social liberalism. All subsequent assessments of the Methodist political tradition were made in the light of this early period of activity.

Unfortunately the development of this branch of Methodism was complicated at an early date by the intrusion of English Wesleyan missionaries. These were drawn to Upper Canada by their interest in Indian missions and by their willingness to assist the provincial government in establishing a loyal, conservative form of Methodism here. To this threat the Canadians responded with an offer of union between the two conferences.

The union took effect in 1833 and remained intact until the parties separated after a blazing row in 1840. By 1847 tempers had cooled sufficiently to permit reunion of the two bodies; this association persisted until the Methodist Church in Canada was formed in 1874.

Although the Canadian Methodists appeared to have been the winners in their long struggle with the Wesleyans, the presence of the latter, in conjunction with changing circumstances, sensibly modified their outlook and their position in Canadian society. With the union the episcopate was abolished, and the presiding elders began to lose ground when they became district chairmen. The conference emerged more clearly as the supreme governing body in the church, but fortunately the distinction between general and annual conferences was retained. There was much talk in those years about conference tyranny, but in reality the ministers became increasingly conscious of lay demands, which they tried to manipulate if not to grant.

In the same period Methodist religious attitudes changed perceptibly. Circuits were supplemented by stations in which a more settled ministry was provided. In urban areas, at least, evangelical zeal became somewhat stereotyped and formal; after 1850 the church began to use professional evangelists. As many developed inhibitions about public confession, the stringent requirement of class meeting attendance came under attack. In effect, the Methodist Church was no longer a body of converts; it was an ongoing community, responsible for the conversion of adults and the spiritual welfare of their children.

It is not surprising that, as the spiritual climate of Canadian Methodism changed, modifications occurred in its views about the secular order. The conference, if not its adherents, was becoming very wary of political entanglements, except those required to protect vital Methodist interests. Although it continued to resist monopoly or favouritism in church-state relations, the conference was now prepared to work with the state and to accept support for Methodist educational institutions. In fact, the vigour with which the Methodists entered into educational controversy is indicative of their continuing concern for the shape of Canadian society. They were still determined to assess its development in the light of their own moral principles and to seek reforms arising out of those principles. They adopted this attitude in part because, of all the Canadian denominations, they were the most nationalist, the most anxious to settle Canadian problems in Canadian terms and the most willing to envisage the parallel expansions of Canada and the Methodist Church.

As the Wesleyan Methodist Church in Canada West grew to maturity, it was faced with growing competition from other Methodist churches. As early as 1829 Primitive Methodism was introduced into Upper Canada, followed by the Bible Christian Church in 1831 and the New Connexion Methodists in 1837. These offshoots of the English Conference appealed to recent immigrants, to those who thought the Canada Conference lukewarm or to those who felt that laymen should help to govern the church. More critical, however, was the organization in 1834 of the Methodist Episcopal Church.

This church, formed initially by those who seceded from the Canada Conference in protest against the 1833 union, professed to represent Methodist orthodoxy in doctrine and polity. It retained the episcopate, fostered close ties with American Methodism, and upheld the evangelical tradition in its narrowest form. Between the Methodist Episcopals and the Wesleyan Methodists a strong antipathy persisted, kept alive by the Episcopals' conviction that they were the true Methodists and by the somewhat contemptuous attitude of the Wesleyans toward them. So long, moreover, as the latter church continued to accommodate itself to changing circumstances, it was bound to throw off discontented elements who found a more comfortable home in the Methodist Episcopal fold.

By the 1860's, then, Methodism had become entrenched in British North America, but its divisions, especially in Canada West, were becoming a source of disquiet. For the observer it was difficult to decide which variety of Methodism was most authentic or most representative. Fortunately the ideal of Methodist unity and the powerful nationalist impulse of the Wesleyan Methodist Church were not dead. Aroused by the example of the provinces themselves, the Methodists moved toward reunion. In 1874 the Wesleyan Methodist Church, the Conference of Eastern British America and the New Connexion Church united to form a new Methodist church. In 1884 the Methodist Episcopal Church and the smaller Methodist churches were incorporated with this church as the Methodist Church, Canada.

IV

To anyone familar with the history of this great new church, its traditions might well have appeared as a collection of fragments. In reality, though, the varieties of Methodism were never so diverse as they seemed. There was a Canadian Methodist "mind"; its essential unity was reflected in the distinctiveness of Methodist ways of seeing and speaking, and its complex evolution was reflected in the nuances of Methodist reactions. Its presence can be illustrated by reference to their religious temper, their views on church government and their vision of the church's place in the world.

To many, the Methodist Church was simply a large and wealthy organization intent upon the protection of its own vested interests.

Undoubtedly this was the real concern of some preachers and perhaps more laymen. Nevertheless, the Methodists as a group held to an evangelical and fundamentalist faith. Inspired by Wesley's example and by the philistinism of their environment, they showed little interest in biblical scholarship; they preferred the literal interpretation of the Scriptures. For them sin and judgment were realities that could be overcome only by a vivid and definite conversion experience. Hence they continued to prefer in principle a type of liturgy and preaching that would disturb the conscience of the participants and bring them to the point of decision. Moreover, they accepted the doctrine of perfection and with it the requirements of regular participation in the means of grace and of love towards neighbours. Probably few claimed the "second blessing," but it was an end toward which all aspired.

Whatever their spiritual guides may have believed—and their thinking became more tolerant and sophisticated after 1900—the likelihood is that most Methodists held these views as late as 1925. Many former Methodists still hold them. But, clearly, there were wide differences in practice between the various sectors of the Methodist community. Many, possibly the majority, preferred services in which the emotional content was high but the real demands low. They cherished warmth, but would have been embarrassed by actual conversions. Yet a substantial minority—especially among rural Methodists, many of whom were former Episcopals—would have responded to a more fervent and more demanding appeal, whereas, at the other extreme, educated urban Methodists sought a more philosophical and more aesthetic type of Christian belief and practice. The result was a constant drain of the dissatisfied either to "holiness" movements or to other churches, leaving behind the most complacent or the least profound.

Fundamental as these spiritual considerations were, the climate of the Methodist polity was also an essential part of the Methodist "mind." By 1900 they had become welded to certain principles of church organization. The general superintendency was an informal episcopate, designed to give leadership and a sense of direction to the church as a whole. There was no evident desire, however, to reproduce in Canada the type of episcopate existing in the Methodist Episcopal Church, U.S.A. Rather the Wesleyan tradition and

Canadian pragmatism had coalesced in a strong antipathy to a genuine episcopate. To most Methodists the Anglican system, for example, was suspect on historical and practical grounds.

Although they were opposed to a strong executive, the Methodists were not really fervent democrats. Naturally they believed that there is no positive distinction between preachers and people; they thought that both should be represented in the government of the church and that the elective principle should prevail. But a Methodist congregation was not a self-contained entity in the same sense as were Baptist or Presbyterian churches. The bias was towards centralization, not local autonomy. Methodists thought it proper that the General Conference should take the initiative and that its actions should be checked by the annual conferences. They agreed that when the majority had decided, the minority should subside and not secede. In effect the Methodist tradition was that neither clergy nor laity should rule absolutely and that neither central nor local interests should dominate each other. The influence of Wesley's autocracy and of the early emergence of the powerful conferences had been modified but not eliminated.

Finally, the Methodists' conception of the proper role of their church in society reflected their religious convictions, their views on church government and their past experience. As in the past, they were driven by their belief that every Christian is responsible for the welfare of his neighbours. In politics, this did not entail identification with any one party. As one might expect, there were liberal and conservative Methodists. It was possible, too, to align large groups of Methodists behind certain politicians simply because they were Methodists. Nevertheless, there was an independent strain in Methodist political behaviour. They could be persuaded to take a critical line, to judge political acts in moral rather than expedient terms—a habit of mind that was often productive of misunderstanding.

What really interested the Methodist Church was the social order and its amelioration. Here again its approach was not always clear-cut. As heirs of an individualist tradition Methodists at first reacted unfavourably to such collective institutions as the trade unions. Similarly, like most religious bodies, they were prone to confuse crime and sin and sought legislation against what they, but not others, considered evils. Yet at their best they were capable of greater and more altruistic deeds. They sought to maintain an intimate connection between Christianity and higher education, but preferred to define this relationship in broad and tolerant terms. Periodically, too, Methodism threw up men who were not afraid to face the ultimate social implications of Christian charity in the contemporary world. It should not be forgotten that the church that produced Albert Carman also produced J. S. Woodsworth. At opposite extremes these men reflected the range of Methodist comprehension of the Christian's proper function in society. Each appealed to elements in the Methodist tradition: Carman to the narrow, individualist ideal of holiness: Woodsworth to the vast social significance of Christian love. That many found it easier to follow men such as Carman should not lead us to underestimate the heights to which they could be led.

On one issue, however, the Methodist position was unambiguous. Although those in the eastern provinces were very conscious of their Wesleyan inheritance, the general outlook of the Methodist community was aggressively Canadian. Perhaps no other Canadian Protestant church had so large a body of native leaders or had become so closely identified with Canadian society. Almost instinctively Methodists dealt with their problems in what were thought to be Canadian ways. Through their all-embracing organization they contributed to the growth of national unity, an end to which they were committed deeply.

V

If the foregoing is a fair account of the contents of the Canadian Methodist "mind," what were its liabilities and assets from the standpoint of the broader Christian world? To those who believed that the Holy Spirit has always acted in a highly selective fashion, Methodism necessarily appeared to be an aberration. Positively, its affinities were with those Christians who have thought that God alone inspires and directs the Christian life, that there is no definitive form of church polity, and that the Christian's duty is to live in the world but not to be of it. Like others who have held similar views, Methodists were rather prone to assert that theirs was the only true faith. Canadian Methodists were not without pride, and they often demonstrated much antipathy to other communions.

It would be wrong, however, to emphasize unduly the denominational element in Canadian Methodism. In other respects it was fitted to play a mediating and uniting part among the churches. Despite the simple fundamentalism of many, the Methodist theological tradition was quite flexible. As Arminians and pragmatists, Methodist theologians particularly were open to new insights and were willing to examine tolerantly other forms of belief. If they did not wholly share Wesley's convictions about the sacraments, they held them in high esteem and were at least potentially able to sympathize with those churches in which they occupied a more important place. Similarly, their conceptions of church government were not rigid. Attached as they were to their own system, they were prepared to consider modification; the operation of their polity was such as to facilitate adjustments. Then, too, as a group that had long been especially concerned with the Christian's duty in the world, they were more willing than others to consider ecclesiastical changes suggested by a rapidly changing intellectual and social scene. As a nationalist body they found it easy to visualize one common form of Christianity for Canada. Frequently this led to an unhealthy confusion of church, society and state, but it was a factor in the union of 1925 and in the continuing interest of the United Church in the unity of Christians in Canada.

Today, although Methodism is a powerful factor in the Christian world, it is but a fading memory in this country. Probably many of those who regret its passing do so for the wrong reasons. Those who would remain faithful to the positive elements in our Methodist tradition would do well to recall that it embodied these fundamental affirmations: Men do not belong to themselves but to God. The Holy Spirit is a living and unfettered reality in the life of the Christian church. There is no one historically valid form of church government. Men who do not seek after holiness will not see God.

7

CHANGING CHARACTERISTICS OF THE CATHOLIC CHURCH

J. A. RAFTIS

The immigration of non-French-speaking Catholics to Canada was not inspired or organized by ecclesiastical purpose after the manner of movements of population in the seventeenth and eighteenth centuries. After an unsuccessful attempt by Lord Baltimore in 1623 to found a religious refuge in Newfoundland with two priests, it would be several generations before the church would be tolerated in that colony so as to allow priests even to appear in public. Only towards the end of the first generation after the British conquest did priests become available in the Maritimes. Prince Edward Island had no priest until 1775; several Irish priests were in Nova Scotia from 1786. In central Canada, English-speaking priests appeared even more slowly. The organized life of the church, especially as represented by the clergy, was not an easily available "import" in the English-speaking world of the late eighteenth and early nineteenth centuries. The demand for religion would have to grow out of the settlements themselves, and in consequence the Canadian church would develop peculiar Canadian problems and characteristics.

To note these obstacles is not to suggest that conditions were largely unfavourable to the growth of the Catholic Church in Canada. Three factors favoured the young English-speaking church. First, the Catholic migrating to Canada in the eighteenth century had the good fortune to find already in existence a well-established French-Canadian church. Political relief tendered to Roman Catholics by the Quebec Act was a pleasant surprise to those emigrating from Ireland and Scotland. Equally important was the missionary spirit of the French-Canadians. From Father Bourg of the Acadians to the pastor at Assumption parish in Sandwich, French-Canadian priests covered the outposts of settlement in the third quarter of the eighteenth century. As the white man moved westward, the French-Canadian priest would be in the vanguard—Provencher and Dumoulin at Red River, the Oblates in the Northwest Territories, Father Demers in British Columbia. This missionary zeal of the French-Canadians underlies the history of the whole of the frontier Catholic Church in Canada.

Secondly, the status permitted Roman Catholics by the Quebec Act of 1774 was not the only indication of an acceptable social and political climate for the new Catholic immigrant. English-speaking Catholics in Canada obtained early favours lightening the burden of the penal laws of the Empire. Bishop Macdonell in Upper Canada and his settled Scots and Irish soldiers had as much title as anyone to the rewards of the United Empire Loyalists. Early support from the British government offset the attractions of the United States, reduced the predominance of the French-speaking bloc, and encouraged the establishment of three apostolic vicariates covering Nova Scotia, New Brunswick, Prince Edward Island, the Magdalen Islands and Upper Canada. In 1826 Alexander Macdonell was consecrated Bishop of Kingston, to found the first Catholic diocese created in a British territory since the Reformation. Bishop Macdonell even accepted an invitation to join the Legislative Council of Upper Canada. Largely from government assistance obtained through this position, he had built thirty-five churches and maintained twenty priests by 1838, whereas in 1804 he had had only three churches and four priests.

A third congenial factor for many a new immigrant was the strong co-operative spirit generated by the frontier. The common poverty of many Catholic and non-Catholic immigrants broke down traditional cultural-religious separatism and exposed all to a common fight for survival. Although there were extreme instances of Catholics being unable to purchase property for a church building, non-Catholic support of subscriptions for the establishment of Catholic parishes is well chronicled. No doubt local civic pride and even economic motives contributed to such assistance as communities became well established, but a native community spirit appeared very early and gave promise of becoming a powerful force in the new society. The rapidity with which the bitter New England sectarian spirit that had provoked the Acadian expulsion was displaced in late-eighteenth-century Nova Scotia is an outstanding case in point. The Nova Scotian tradition of harmony between separate and public schools is one of the most significant products of this native co-operative spirit.

The Roman Catholic Church was not destined to grow steadily from these favourable conditions. Immigration gradually reduced dependence upon the French-Canadian church, undermined the quasi-establishment sought by Bishop Macdonell, and perpetuated the emergency conditions of the frontier. The gradual decline in strength of the French-Canadian church is most easily charted by the withdrawal of government support for French schools: in New Brunswick, from 1871; Ontario, 1911; Manitoba, 1890; British Columbia in the third quarter of the nineteenth century; the North-west Territories in 1892 and 1901. From this increasingly defensive position the French-Canadian church was less and less able to give leadership to the English-speaking body. In return, however, the fact that the bulk of the first non-French Catholic immigrants were English-speaking Irish facilitated the growth of the Roman Catholic Church in an Anglo-Saxon culture. Macdonell was not the last ardent British patriot among Catholic bishops, as Bishop Fallon of London showed during World War I.

As Irish immigration reached massive proportions, Irish traditions began to be imported in their entirety to the Canadian church. Some Irish immigrants were as willing to oppose the establishment of either Anglican or Catholic churches as were the evangelical sects. The bitter orange-versus-green incidents that rocked the country from one end to the other in the 1850's were a direct result of large-scale immigration. The intensity of pamphlet-inflamed public opinion over this period subverted the tranquillity of many a local community and turned the minds of the people more and more towards political organization as an instrument of co-operation or failure to co-operate. But if religion had to work through politics, it is noteworthy that politics never became simply religion. Most indicative of this, perhaps, is the fact that lists of both federal and provincial members of Parliament from Ontario over the past one hundred years find Catholics fairly equally in the ranks of both parties.

The mass immigration of the nineteenth century demonstrated

that the structure of the church, evolved over the centuries under all kinds of conditions, is remarkably flexible despite its formidable canonical framework. Rome's readiness to create new missionary territories (vicariates), or to subdivide dioceses for the sake of a few thousand persons served by a handful of priests, is repeatedly manifested in the history of Canada. The chart of new parishes and dioceses follows closely the growth and movements of populations.

No amount of efficiency in ecclesiastical organization was able to compensate, however, for the lack of men and resources on the frontier. The suddenness of immigration, the impermanence of many settlements and the difficulties of communication militated against the simple transplantation and growth of European diocesan organization. Until the second quarter of the nineteenth century the inadequacy of trade, communications and currency made the establishment of parishes a precarious business. Between 1850 and 1930 large-scale immigration to Canada was balanced by equal emigration from Canada. Migration within Canada was an equally disturbing factor, as when the "Saugeen fever" filled the Georgian Bay area after 1850 or when western Canada attracted thousands of easterners at the end of the century. Some parish churches in older settlements never progressed or had to be abandoned for lack of priests, parishioners or resources. Frontier parishes were often torn by dissension, whether over the location of the church, the title to the church property or the assessment for parochial expenditures. Factions and the personality of priests might precipitate such issues, but the underlying problem was the underdeveloped frontier with its shortage of money, its reaction against too much organization and its educational disabilities resulting in simple ignorance of the rudiments of the ecclesiastical structure. Clergy had to gauge the frontier condition and spirit with realism, and perhaps a few bishops and not a few priests foundered in their administration and retired through failure to do so. But the spirit developed by the frontier environment, rough, gross and materialistic as it was, purged a vacuous sophistication and secular cynicism inherited from eighteenth-century Europe. The immigrant was usually willing to make great sacrifices to found his place of worship in the New World.

The lack of confreres to ease the burden or work and isolation shortened the working lives of many early diocesan priests. In many

areas the turnover of priests, especially until the middle of the nineteenth century, was even more drastic than shifts in population.
Resources of missionary orders were called upon to meet this chronic
emergency. In many districts Jesuits, Oblates or Redemptorists supplied spiritual ministrations for generations. To some degree the
frontier hurdle was eased by the ability of religious to draw upon
European resources, as in the case of money collected in Europe for
the foundation of churches in Waterloo County, Ontario, by Father
Holzer S.J. Equally well adapted to the frontier was the "revival"
technique of missions conducted by such missionary clergy—stressing
excesses of life, compensating for irregular instructions, appealing to
the whole community:

We began the exercises of the Mission on the 29th of August, the
Feast of the Immaculate Heart of Mary. The large attendance and
the smallness of the church obliged us to preach in the open air. This
we did four times daily. The success obtained surpassed our most
sanguine expectations. Whole families came on foot, on horseback
and in oxen wagons from great distances. On the second and third
days many went home twelve to thirty miles to bring their families
and neighbours. One who had come just for the Sunday on account
of pressing work, went home during the night and brought his family
and friends the next day, and stayed until the close of the Mission.
Then he was sorry that it was over. Even the most urgent work of
harvesting was left undone. People seemed insensible to hunger,
thirst, and rest. Many who had for years refused to go to confession
came before daybreak and besieged the confessional for hours until
they could enter it. At the close of the Mission a large cross 26 feet
high, that was carried on the shoulders of the young men to its
place was erected in the cemetery. What sweet joy filled all hearts
on seeing the sign of Salvation erected on the hill dominating the
whole district!   (New Germany, August, 1847)

While a religious community is "organized stability," it was
equally the stable Christian culture that supplied the greatest
number of vocations and the greatest material resources to the
growing Catholic Church in Canada. The large number of clergy and
religious from Ireland in the nineteenth century has been paralleled
by the importance of priests and bishops from the Maritimes for the
church right across Canada in the twentieth century. As the bulk of
Catholics in eastern Canada became urban, however, a more
organized recruitment of such resources became necessary. With the

spread of the missionary frontier all over the west in the twentieth century, the Catholic Church Extension Society organized men and money for this work.

The historical life of the Catholic Church is more than the story of priests and the dispensation of spiritual services. Christianity attempts to inspire the whole community with its spirit, and so from Christian society emerge myriad organizations with charitable, educational and social purposes. A frontier church would obviously tend to import this whole structure of organization. Pious parochial societies at first imitated the pattern of nineteenth-century Europe, focusing largely on service to the parish church through such groups as altar societies and Christian family organizations. The elemental conditions of the new country called for immediate services, however; after parish churches came orphanages, hospitals and homes for the aged, as well as schools. The Sisters of St. Joseph, the Grey Nuns, the Sisters of St. Ann and other sisterhoods moved across Canada in the wake of the first missionaries. Charity, the highest expression of Christian life, tends by the very essence of the charitable act to escape the historian's calculus. The impact of even organized Christian charity on the formation of American civilization is probably the least studied of any aspect of the history of the church. While the importation of varied Christian denominations created a hazard for the establishment of a Canadian community, the binding service of charity breached many religious differences. Bigots might be sensitive to privilege, and politicians would argue over rights, but the services of Catholic hospitals and hundreds of dedicated religious were extended to the whole community. It is perhaps sufficient to say here that the persistence of dozens of pioneer charitable institutions through the involvements of industrialization, the sophistication of urbanization and the growing services of the welfare state bears witness to the unique contribution made by this facet of the life of the church.

The Catholic Church in Canada was fortunate in being able to draw upon the great religious revival in Europe after the Napoleonic Wars. To restored seventeenth-century foundations such as the Redemptorists, Christian Brothers and Sisters of Loretto were added early nineteenth-century foundations such as the Resurrectionists, Oblates and Basilians. The Canadian church would have taken generations to produce the leadership and expertise imported with these institutions. Yet the number of persons coming from Europe was very limited, the success of a particular institution depending very much upon its immediate and fairly rapid increase by native recruitment. This combination of imported format and native vitality was bound to precipitate crises. In some organizations, such as the Sisters of St. Joseph, growth by separation off along the lines of diocesan structures proved to be an admirable principle of development. Where societies were less dedicated to immediate practical works of charity, traditions were more formidable. This proved particularly to be the case in congregations dedicated to education, where crises forced one community after another to separate from Europe by provinces or even to form distinct canonical societies. On the other hand, the growth of a diocesan clergy tended to indicate the full maturing of a native religious cultural tradition through a fixed and stable population. Religious communities tended to be outward-looking because of their identification with some function in the church, whether charity, education, preaching or a particular devotion. But the stable maturity of Maritime society from the mid-nineteenth century, and of that of central Canada from later in the century, were both marked by a rapid strengthening in numbers and training of the diocesan clergy.

Catholic primary education in Canada quickly passed from the initial stage of private masters' schools to that of organized board schools resembling more or less closely the free common schools. Though their early history is the record of one controversy after another, of alignment now with this now with that political or religious faction, the Catholic separate schools have shared from the beginning in the general victory of public tax-supported schools over the presumed prerogatives of the schools of the Establishment, improperly so called. In Ontario and the Maritimes, Catholic primary schools succeeded in getting, during the middle decades of the nineteenth century, the kind of foothold that political Confederation was both to confirm and to legalize. Since Confederation there has been a tendency on the part of Catholic primary schools to offer a programme paralleling that of the public schools. Thus, while on the one hand they have been confessional and have operated under religious auspices, at the same time they have been part of the public school system and have provided comparable facilities and comparably, even similarly, qualified teachers. The resemblances at this level between Catholic schools and public schools have over the years been perhaps more significant than the differences.

At the secondary level the story has been different. Most Catholic secondary schools were, in the beginning, called "colleges." This was partly in emulation of the privately endowed Protestant colleges on the English public school pattern, partly in imitation of the French *collège*, whose academic programme they usually adopted. Some of the first Catholic secondary schools were founded by French religious. These were much less high schools than "Little Seminaries," and they were expected to supply the church with native Canadian vocations. The relation between their academic programmes and those of the public high schools was in the beginning at least one of sharp contrast. Since the Catholic population of Canada was not university-minded, these secondary schools or colleges were generally accepted as "institutions of higher learning." They did not operate under provincial departments of education, sought no departmental recognition, and demanded no formal qualifications of their staffs. Within the general educational scheme, they represented a break with the principle of conformity that was more or less accepted at the primary level. The history of Catholic secondary education in the twentieth century is the record of the transformation of the Little Seminaries into matriculation schools.

Catholic universities in the full sense have not existed in English-speaking Canada until within the last twenty years. The more successful colleges developed arts courses leading to recognized B.A. degrees, but none succeeded in establishing the costly professional faculties. They even lacked formally erected faculties of theology. Interesting, however, has been the affiliation and federation of certain Catholic colleges with provincial universities, providing a kind of return at the highest level to the principle of academic conformity achieved long before in the primary schools.

A number of significant factors have been operative in Catholic education at all three levels: the constant pressure of clergy and laity for more and more "vocations"; the demand at the same time for leaders in professional life and for directors of social activities; a general willingness to put up with a minimal supply of books and other essential tools of scholarship; a preoccupation with institutional prestige in competitive sports; a desire that Catholic education function within the tax structure of municipal and provincial governments.

It can be noted too that in Canada, in Catholic as well as in non-Catholic communities, there has been a more vigorous attachment to education in settlements of predominantly Scottish background; that noteworthy achievements in education have usually been attributable to individuals rather than to groups; and that there has been a strong awareness within the Catholic constituency that their schools have never really moved out of pioneer conditions. Perhaps it is the feeling that these conditions are now being left behind that sounds the new note in Catholic education.

No doubt the lack of industrialization long isolated the Canadian church from many elements growing in her American counterpart. It did not seem of decisive importance to the English-speaking Canadian of the 1880's that the French-Canadian hierarchy would have the Knights of Labour condemned whereas the American church, under the leadership of Cardinal Gibbons, could vindicate this right of labour to organize. Even by the time of the Great Depression of the 1930's, Canadian efforts on behalf of the worker were but a pale reflection of the labour schools in American Catholic colleges. The justly world-famous co-operative work sponsored by the Extension Department of St. Francis Xavier University, Antigonish, made noticeably less impact upon industrialized than upon rural areas. None the less, as industrialization has progressed in Canada the American rather than the European church has provided the model for organization. Although the organized hierarchial approach to social questions, represented in the United States by the National Catholic Welfare Conference founded after World War I, would be paralleled in Canada only after World War II with the founding of the Canadian Catholic Council, the model is obvious. On the whole, however, the impact of the United States upon the Canadian Catholic Church is much less than upon many other Canadian cultural areas. This statement holds true for both positive and negative influences. By and large the Canadian Catholic has not committed his resources to the support of the church as generously as has his American fellow-Catholic. At the same time he has been spared many of the bitter sectarian attacks made upon his fellow-Catholics in the United States, and efforts to attack Catholics under the badge of religious nationalism of the APA variety have not been prolonged in a nation with such a large Catholic population.

The distinctive educational situation of the Catholic Church in Canada has provided the main obstacle to disturbing American influences. As cultural formation moves out of the hands of the educators, however, the American impact becomes more marked. The full meaning of the common North American radio and television audience is as yet difficult to assess in the religious area, but the intrusion of American public relations organization has been strongly felt over the past two decades in such activities as fundraising and tithing. Those powerful forces in modern society that bring Catholic, Protestant and Jew together in the "American way of life" described by Will Herberg are now clearly at work in Canada. In part, this is only evidence of a new co-operative culture, and such activities as the Red Feather campaign may be compared with the co-operative ventures of the frontier. If Herberg's suggestion that this development is a common adoration of a standard of living is valid, the theological significance of such co-operation is far to seek. Undoubtedly, however, there *is* a theological inspiration for co-operation in the field of social action, and much common ground between the social doctrine of the World Council of Churches and that of the Papal Social Encyclicals is gradually being revealed. As labour leader, capitalist and politician increasingly recognize the necessity for a new social ethic in the welfare world, it becomes of more pressing importance that Christians find common intellectual as well as practical areas of co-operation. Canadians have been spared much of the suspicion of Catholic Action now rampant in Australia largely because of the small impact of Catholic social thought in highly industrialized areas. It may be noted, however, that the recent conservative reaction among American Catholics has found a strong sympathy in Canada.

Here again the problem of education comes to the fore. Catholic lay organizations are inspired today by a more positive purpose than the "defence of the faith" approach encouraged by Pope Leo XIII in the nineteenth century, although that approach was typical of such nineteenth-century foundations as the Knights of Columbus until within the past few years. With a common system of education, a growing professional class and the increased recognition of "planning" forces at work on every level of society, a more positive spirit is to be discovered today in both old and new lay organizations. The Christian Family Movement and the Young Christian Workers represent such new organizations. It is generally acknowledged that these new activities must develop in two directions: 1) through more mature theological training in order that the members may represent the church and yet not identify the spiritual and temporal; and 2) through greater practical co-operation with non-Catholic groups so that the common good of a pluralistic society may be furthered.

From the end of the nineteenth century, and particularly since World War I, the changing pattern of immigration and increasing industrialization have gradually multiplied and intensified many characteristics of earlier generations. Bishops of several rites, churches of a wide number of languages, priests and religious of a a remarkable variety of cultures and communities, now answer to the needs of the immigrant. The problem of national culture and Canadian Catholicism varies with the nationality. Among some groups, such as the Poles and Ukrainians, many former difficulties of the French-Canadian have been repeated: they have sought a close identification of culture, language and religion simply because of a historical memory that political conquest and cultural domination meant loss of religion. To others no such identification seems necessary. Just as Canada posed no great problem for the Irish in the nineteenth century because they had already learned to preserve their faith through the English language, so large Latin immigrant groups in the twentieth century are insensitive to the impact of cultural change upon faith because they have no tradition of a threat to religion through cultural dominance.

Even in the extremely mobile conditions of the mid-twentieth century, the national parish and indeed the national diocese have been important foci for immigrants. But more important in the rapid urbanization since World War II has been the attraction of the parochial school for young Catholic parents, who are anxious for the future of their children in the insecure city and are more willing to align themselves publicly with religious education in a world that faces the threat of atheistic communism. There are increasing signs that over the next generation the Roman Catholic laity will be in many ways more sensitive than the clergy to the necessity for Catholic education. This will be an important factor in the survival of this system of education, for the laity are gradually assuming major responsibility for it. The popularity of lay retreats and an increasing concern for a theology for the laity are other facets of a new pattern in the church of the twentieth century. Some developments echo the nineteenth-century tradition of the frontier. Religious priests are again proving to be the most readily available resource for new national groups. The unstable conditions of urban parochial life are once more encouraging an emphasis upon the more devotional evangelical thought and practice. The Rosary Crusade of Father Peyton and the devotions to Our Lady of Fatima are new forms of this nineteenth-century missionary revival. At the same time the growing "liturgical revival" is gradually setting the tone for devotional practice; it bids fair to provide the parish church with a more adequate spiritual focus in the community.

8

LUTHERAN TRADITION IN CANADA

WALTER FREITAG

Formidable obstacles confront anyone who would study Lutheran tradition in Canada. An historical investigation is indispensable to our inquiry. Despite invaluable contributions to the history of Lutheranism in this country, however, no complete history is yet available. We are therefore face to face with a methodological problem of the first magnitude. How are we to proceed with our investigation?

In order to meet the difficulties inherent in the problem—and perhaps to outflank them—I propose to borrow a discipline from another field of endeavour and to adapt it to our purpose. This discipline, called ecology, is the science that treats of plants and animals in reference to their environment and to the factors that control or have controlled their distribution. In our context, let us define an ecological study as an inquiry into the setting of Lutheranism in Canada inclusive of factors deemed formative for tradition.

At the outset, it is imperative for us to gain some insight into the configuration of Lutheranism in this land. The Lutheran Church is not a foreign church. It is not a national church. It is not an indigenous church. But it is at the same time foreign, national and indigenous.

The shaping of this enigma may have been predetermined by certain decisions taken at the time of the Reformation. The Lutheran Church of that day refused to allow organizational structure to become an essential feature of its genius. Tradition also was denied that privileged status. The reason for these actions was not the relegation of polity and tradition to the realm of the inconsequential but the divorcement of both from the iron grip of ecclesiastical imperialism.

But the consequences following upon these decisions make us wonder. Were not polity and tradition in fact subjected to other pressures no less dangerous than those of ecclesiastical ambition? The question is of some moment. When we look at the mosaic of Lutheran church polity on the continent, no uniform pattern of development is obvious. The employment of the territorial principle in Germany illustrates one pattern, but the modification of the diocesan structure in the Scandinavian countries is indicative of another pattern. The forces urging national identity and later moulding the state-church relationship may be said to have been predictable.

At the same time as the churches were moving in the direction of national self-consciousness and closer relationships with the state, counter-movements were also gathering momentum. These were movements concerned about the spiritual life of the people, who were worried about social conditions and wary of political entanglements. In some nations the church learned the wisdom of keeping these vital movements within itself. In others it did not, and time served to mould them into churches existing independently of the state church. The lack of a common design in the founding of the Lutheran churches in Europe tends to substantiate our postulate.

But what happened in Canada? The settlers who populated this land brought with them the heritage of their homelands. We should naturally have expected that colonists from the same country in a particular area would have sought some kind of relationship with the parent church. Ordinarily this did not happen, however, and when it did the connection was of brief duration. Whatever the reason, many immigrants desired no such tie; for others, one was not possible since their homeland was no more; for those to whom it was of some moment, the multiple factors of distance, climate, adverse living conditions and poor communication militated heavily against any realization of their hopes. Nor can we gainsay the fact that the brute force required just to stay alive in the new country consumed both passion and energy. In summary, the immigrants who made this land their home invested it with the customs and traditions they cherished, adapting no more than was necessary for compatibility with the rigours of existence here.

Lutheranism in this context was parochial and international under the pressure of the indigenous.

Not all immigrants to Canada arrived via the port of Halifax. Many came by way of the United States, and a significant number came as immigrants from that country. In the course of time, the settlements of Lutherans in Canada entered into organic relationship with Lutheran church bodies in the republic. A new dimension was thus introduced into our setting. In order to appreciate it, however, we must briefly review the ecology of Lutheranism in the great republic.

The Lutheran churches in the United States did not take shape along the line of the territorial principle or the diocesan or even that of the free church. They came into existence in order to minister to specific constituencies: the Augustana Synod to serve the needs of the Swedish people, the Haugean to minister to the Norwegian pietist community, etc. Interestingly, due to language barriers among many other factors, these historical developments took place with little reference to, or knowledge of, what was happening among Lutherans elsewhere in the nation.

As the several church bodies moved toward indigeneity, the possibilities for inter-Lutheran discussion became ever more tantalizing. Consultations began, merger negotiations followed, and new alignments were consummated. These successive mergers have drastically reduced the numbers of Lutheran churches in the United States. This represents a remarkable if not unparalleled achievement.

The Canadian counterpart to this story presents some surprising features. Mergers produced realignments in jurisdictional units in this country also, but with a difference. For example, whereas The United Lutheran Church in America, the American Evangelical Lutheran Church, the Augustana Synod and the Suomi Synod were party to the recent merger resulting in the Lutheran Church in America, only the first and third of these are significantly represented in Canada. Still more intriguing is the fact that these two had both been members of an earlier Lutheran grouping, the General Council, prior to the merger in 1918 that produced The United Lutheran Church of America. A process similar to that just illustrated took place in the other synods or districts of the Lutheran churches in Canada at the time of their respective mergers. One consequence of this is that the Canadian units generally represent the more conservative wing of the parent organizations in the United States. Thus we have American Lutheranism superimposed upon that of the continent, while the blend has occasioned certain characteristics that may fairly be described as Canadian.

In this context, tradition is almost impossible to describe. If tradition is defined as that which is handed down from generation to generation, having in the process acquired the character of duration, and if the specifically theological is excluded from the scope of this inquiry, then it must be said that there is no tradition common to Lutheranism in Canada. There may be traditions in the several jurisdictional units of Lutheran churches in Canada, but these have not yet become unalterable. We may also find that there are some factors having a formative effect upon tradition. But there is not yet any common tradition.

It would serve no fruitful purpose to attempt to excise the traditions of the components of Canadian Lutheranism from the tangled web in which they are embedded. Indeed, such an analysis would merely accentuate our dilemma. We will, therefore, look at the formative factors affecting tradition.

As we have already suggested, Lutherans are free to address themselves to any given situation, to the issues involved, and to the persons or corporate bodies thereto related, without any necessary prior reference to tradition or precedent. Operationally speaking, the Lutheran Church normally fulfils these functions in and through congregations. It thus has the potential capability of expressing its confessional genius anew in each particular situation.

As a result, Lutheran practice allows for considerable latitude and flexibility in its address to problematic situations in such areas as manners and morals, polity and administration, education and worship, society and culture. Since no two situations are alike, one will find within the confines of Lutheranism virtually every conceivable position on such matters. In one case it may take a position that would otherwise be described as legalistic, in another a liberal stance, in still another a conservative posture. In one instance it may support a temperance movement, while in another it may defend the alcoholic from abuse. In one setting it may foster a highly liturgical worship service, in another the so-called "free" service. It could even change its position on the same problem within the same community if the situation itself changed. All this points to a highly significant observation, namely, that the apparent rigidity of Lutherans in their confessional posture is functionally dynamic in fact.

The crucial difficulty raised for Lutheranism by its freedom of expression is the danger either of procrastination or of unreflective dependance upon precedent. Over against this risk, however, we must set the responsibility that this very freedom imposes. In general, it may be said that accountability for actions taken requires careful judgment no less than cautious execution. No wonder that tradition is often considered suspect, especially since it carries within itself an inner momentum toward fixity. At the risk of over-simplification, we may affirm that Lutheranism will tolerate much as long as the confessional tradition is not despised and matters are dealt with in decency and good order. Despite great diversity of opinion, the ethical stance of Lutherans is, if not identical, markedly congruent.

In order to be articulately relevant in its address to modern-day problems both within and outside of the church, Lutherans have traditionally concerned themselves with the education of their youth. Though the materials and methods may vary, Lutheran children are subjected to a rather rigorous process of instruction in the faith for a considerable number of years. The church also has a vested interest in higher education, and urges its young people to prepare adequately for their various vocations. It further insists upon a highly educated ministry; in our time it has consistently been raising the standards of admission to its theological institutions.

If we take these factors into account, it becomes possible to indicate the direction in which Lutheranism is moving in Canada. We need some caution here, however, for in its historical development Lutheranism in this country has gone through two distinct phases.

In its first phase Lutheranism was largely confined to eastern Canada. Here it has enjoyed a continuous history of two centuries and is now practically indigenous, although relationships with corporate entities in the United States are still maintained. In contrast with the more recent history of Lutheranism in western Canada, its setting is comparatively uniform and homogenous.

The second phase, in the West, was initiated before the building of the Canadian Pacific Railway by emigration to Canada by boat down the Red River to Winnipeg. The history of the Lutheran communities in the prairie regions is extremely complex. Records indicate that Lutheran churches ministered to people of a dozen nationalities and did so in at least seven languages. American or other parent bodies serving this varied constituency numbered at one point at least nine. Happily, this number has recently been reduced by mergers to three. The fact that the period spanned is much less than half that in eastern Canada indicates the chasm between East and West.

I think that one can distinguish in Canadian Lutheranism three general types of churchmanship, one or more of which may be found in each of the jurisdictional units.

The first of these may be described as the "low church" movement. It is characterized by the so-called "free" service, simple appointments, the absence of clerical vestments, the use of lay readers and the like. The adherents of this position have usually come under the persuasive influence of pietist movements that emphasize the reading of Scripture, the practice of prayer and pious exercise. In addition, due largely to certain experiences in history, these people have adopted an attitude against culture (to borrow a phrase from Richard Niebuhr) that is expressed in a suspicion of intellectualism and a stark code of behaviour.

The second expression of Lutheranism may be considered the pristine form. Members of this group represent the ultra-conservative wing. They are the most inflexible in matters of doctrine if not always of practice. They have a well-developed form of worship, tasteful appointments, a minimum of vestments. They are characterized by a deep interest in the indoctrination of their youth and in the task of missions. Especially in moral questions their general stance is against culture, their orthodoxy fostering an attitude of exclusiveness.

The third group may be called the moderates. They are characterized by a rather highly developed form of worship, proper appointments and more extensive use of vestments. They are influenced by a mild piety and by an ethical posture more amenable to harmony between church and culture.

It must be repeated, with deliberate emphasis, that no single jurisdictional unit exclusively represents any single one of these expressions. In fact, no one expression of Lutheranism is free of admixture from another. The convergence of certain factors points toward the formation of traditions having these characteristics, but the process of formation is still far from complete.

During the past decade there has been an increasing rapprochement among the Lutheran churches in Canada, especially by way of the Canadian Lutheran Council. This agency was brought into existence to provide certain services that could not be provided by the synods or districts themselves. One Lutheran group did not associate itself with this venture at the time of its inauguration, but events as recent as September, 1962, indicate that a new inter-service agency, inclusive of all Lutherans in Canada, will be brought into being in the near future. Besides dealing with such concerns as social welfare, relief, and college and university work, the Canadian Lutheran Council has become a meeting ground for Lutherans in Canada. By facilitating mutual recognition of the several churches in areas of common effort, it has led them to closer relationships with each other.

As has been noted in other studies, Lutherans and other Protestant churches began their existence in this country by serving people of the lower class. This in itself required of the churches a considerable adjustment in their total conception of the work of the church. In the process of time, however, the situation has changed. Today there is a new configuration, some features of which are unlike any in previous history.

It is becoming increasingly imperative for the Lutheran churches of this country so to organize themselves that their boundaries will be conterminous with those of the nation and, beyond that, to move towards a unified expression of that for which the Lutheran Church stands. At this writing, all of the jurisdictional units of the Lutheran churches either are, or have been granted the right to become, autonomous in Canada. We may expect to see rapid development in this direction within the present decade.

To return to the basic thesis, the Lutheran Church in Canada is neither foreign, national nor indigenous. It is at the same time foreign,

46358

national and indigenous. What applies to it also applies to Lutheran tradition.

What has been said in the foregoing can be challenged at nearly every point. There are so many exceptions in each instance that the thread of continuity is hard to perceive. But I trust that those readers who are intimately acquainted with the history of Lutheranism in Canada will exercise forbearance in a measure appropriate to the theme.

9

CANADIAN ORTHODOXY AND
THE UNION OF CHURCHES

MILOS MLADENOVIC

I

In Canada the division of Christian believers into different churches did not appear as the result of an original process within the country but was brought here as an established pattern by the settlers from their homelands along with their historical and emotional attitudes. Under the influence of local conditions in Canada the pattern changed somewhat. In the case of the Orthodox churches, however, these changes usually did not cause the emergence of fundamentally different Orthodox communities, nor did they bring about the amalgamation of Orthodox communities with other churches except in the case of the Ukrainian Independent Greek Church which joined the Presbyterian Church in 1913.

For the same reason, different representatives of Orthodox churches have taken different attitudes towards the ecumenical movement ranging from accentuated caution to hopeful expectancy, many of them feeling that the existing situation has been very detrimental not only to their churches and the lives of their ethnic groups in Canada but also, on a higher level, to Christianity as a whole. At the beginning the idea of the union of churches was sincerely greeted by the Orthodox. As the work of the movement progressed, however, their interest began to concentrate on the question of the character of the international church meetings and on the problem of future relationships on doctrinal grounds among three traditions: Orthodox, Protestant and Roman.

Through Protestant initiative, the ecumenical movement began as an action by individuals. It became the "World Council of Churches," a title that cannot be accepted by the Orthodox Church because of the term "churches." According to the Orthodox there is only one indivisible church, and that is the Orthodox Church.[1] It was necessary to make a special draft in order to make it possible for the Orthodox to join the World Council of Churches. The Declaration of Toronto specified in 1950 that a member church was not necessarily supposed to consider other churches as "churches" in the full sense of the word. The Orthodox stand was clarified in 1954 at Evanston, where in connection with the Faith and Order report the Orthodox delegates issued a special statement in which they proclaimed that the separated religious communities "are lacking certain basic elements which contribute to the fulness of the Church" and should return to the "faith of the ancient, united and indivisible Church of the Seven Ecumenical Councils." In 1960, when the report of The Faith and Order Commission was adopted at St. Andrews in Scotland, the Orthodox delegation stressed again that the ecumenical problem is that of the Protestant world, and that the main question is that of "denominationalism," which is that of schism. At the meetings of the Council, the Orthodox and the Protestants do not always see the same reality, even when they use the same terms.[2]

Furthermore, neither the Christian ecumenical movement nor the World Council of Churches is universal, and the international meetings are not truly ecumenical in character because of the absence of the Roman Church. Representatives of the Orthodox Church in Canada regret extremely that the Roman Church does not take part in these inter-ecclesiastical discussions. Instead of sending observers, they say, the Roman Church should participate in the work of the Council, for only in this way can the ecumenical character of the meetings be secured. Real attempts towards a successful union of churches might then be undertaken, mutual understanding between the two churches which both claim to be the one and only indivisible Christian Church could develop, and a solution to the main problem in their relationship—the role of the local episcopate in its relation to the see of Rome—could perhaps be found. It is here that we meet the fundamental division between Rome and Orthodoxy.

The latest Vatican Council is considered by Orthodoxy to be predominantly an internal gathering of the Roman prelates. It is felt to

[1]J. Meyendorff, "The Orthodox Concept of the Church," *St. Vladimir's Seminary Quarterly*, Vol. 6 (1962), No. 2, p. 68.
[2]Statement by the Orthodox delegation in the Section on Unity, *St. Vladimir's Seminary Quarterly*, Vol. 6 (1962), No. 1, p. 40.

have no bearing on the united efforts of other churches towards union, not only because of its character but also because one can expect as positive results only the clarification of existing conditions in the practices of the Roman Church in different parts of the world rather than measures that give hope for future co-operation with the ecumenical movement.

II

Discussions touching upon aspects of the doctrine and the inner discipline of the churches are to be expected by clergymen and laymen of the Orthodox churches in Canada. For the time being, their attitudes are sometimes cautious, sometimes intransigent. Thus a representative of the Serbian Orthodox Church in Canada, comparing the Protestant, Orthodox and Roman churches, concluded that the Orthodox doctrine represents a golden mean, whereas the Roman Church tends towards the extreme right and the Protestant churches towards the extreme left. He added, "If there ever be a reunion in essence it must be achieved—we humbly confess—by an opposite way of two extremes moving."[1]

With respect to doctrine, the Canadian Orthodox churches, together with their sister churches in the United States, with which the majority of them are in association, follow the general leadership of the Orthodox churches outside this continent. The directions taken so far do not seem to be very promising, but the situation is not entirely discouraging. The discussions have only just begun, and they are still at a stage where presuppositions have to be clarified to allow any real work of interpretation to begin. So far, reports represent mainly traditional attitudes. In the meantime the world has undergone tremendous changes which have produced new needs and opened up new perspectives, some of them of frightening proportions. These new challenges have thrown a new light upon our old truths. Representatives of the churches have to be guided by these new circumstances and divest themselves of historical differences and prejudices in order to meet the exigencies of human life in this new era.

[1]D. Najdanovich, "The Golden Mean," *Orthodoxy*, Year II (1962), No. 3, p. 12.

In addition to posing questions in the domain of dogma, the new challenges are believed to be imposing upon the Orthodox churches in Canada a demand for more efficient co-operation in the form of territorial organization that would synchronize and consolidate their efforts. Past experiences must be taken into consideration if the difficulties encountered by the Canadian Orthodox churches in this domain are to be understood and removed.

III

The major denominations in Canada succeeded in bringing territorial churches into being either because their administration was centralized or because the majority of their members were originally of the same nationality. Sometimes both factors worked together, as in the case of the Roman Church in French-speaking Canada. The Orthodox, however, were followers of various national churches. Small in number and scattered over the huge expanse of Canada, members of particular ethnic groups had to wait for a long time before the influx of a sufficient number of new immigrants enabled them to set up even local religious communities.[1]

Up to that moment, these isolated immigrants were forced to join other churches or at least to take part in the worship of other religious communities. In choosing another church, they were in general guided by what they had known in their countries of origin. A Russian, for instance, was influenced neither by the internal relations between Catholics and Protestants nor by the practical consequences of the conflict between the Catholics and Orthodox; he was, therefore, not inhibited from participating in the worship of one church or the other. Other Orthodox Christians preferred to keep away from the Roman and Reformed churches and found refuge in the Anglican Church, which had had warm relations with the Orthodox Church since their first contacts in the nineteenth century and the beginning of the twentieth.

Attendance at other churches was only a temporary solution for the individual Orthodox Christian. When Orthodox immigrants of the same ethnic origin increased in number, they were no longer

[1] H. H. Walsh, "The Christian Heritage in Canada," *Canadian Journal of Theology*, Vol. VII (1961), No. 4, p. 279.

satisfied with the prevailing situation and tried to organize their own religious community. The Russians already had on the North American continent an established tradition with regard to their own church, a church that had been kept alive despite a chequered history, but other Orthodox Christians had to start afresh. Many of these communities, unable at first to erect their own houses of worship, were forced to hold their services in private homes or in churches of other religious communities. The true spirit of Christianity was fully expressed in the help so generously given to new religious communities by existing churches, especially by the American Episcopalian and the Canadian Anglican churches. There was also mutual support between certain Slavonic churches where racial affinities and in some instances warm feelings of friendship played important roles in supplementing the testimony of the Christian spirit.

Nevertheless, such co-operation was limited. Feelings of Slavonic solidarity and exacting experiences in a new country, where mutual support is of decisive advantage for overcoming the difficulties of adjustment, did not prevent various ethnic groups from developing isolated societies that served as conservators of old-country customs and historical prejudices. This development favoured the habit, familiar in Eastern Christendom, of setting up territorial churches on an ethnic basis. Although contrary to the Canadian pattern, this practice was beneficial to uprooted immigrants suffering from psychological and spiritual instability. It helped them to adjust themselves to their new cultural surroundings, to regain their personal security and to resist the temptations of some fundamentalist sects. Stundists, Jehovah's Witnesses and Seventh-Day Adventists may be found among the Slavs, especially among the Ukrainians.[1] These had been deserting state Orthodoxy already at home, where defection had a quality of nationalism, as it still had in Canada.[2] But the origins of nonconformism and sectarianism have mainly to be sought in the great Russian schism (*Raskol*) of the seventeenth century, when the gate had been opened for all those who searched for religious freedom and social justice.[3]

[1]C. H. Young, *The Ukrainian Canadians* (Toronto, 1931), p. 148.
[2]I. F. Mackinnon, *Canada and the Minority Churches of Eastern Europe, 1946-1950* (Halifax, N.S., 1959), p. 150.
[3]S. Bolshakoff, *Russian Nonconformity* (Philadelphia, 1949), p. 46.

IV

Some other factors, such as the Russian Revolution and violent changes in the social and political systems of eastern European nations, represented and still represent disruptive forces not only among various national groups but even within some of them.

Despite its tradition in America, the Russian Orthodox Church was unable to overcome its condition of disorganization and pass on to that of reorientation. The first Russian congregations were formed at the beginning of this century and came under the primacy of the Russian Orthodox Church of North America. This church had been established in Alaska in 1794, and after the sale of Alaska to the United States it had been transferred first to San Francisco and then to New York. The Russian Church endeavoured to take care of all Orthodox Christians who had no church of their own in Canada, but it had difficulties with a false metropolitan in 1903 and 1904, with the Doukhobors,[1] a sect of the Russian Old Believers who did not want to have anything to do with the official Russian church, and with the Uniates, who in the absence of their own clergymen wavered between the Russian Orthodox Church and the local Catholic Church.

Nevertheless, the Russian Church of Canada as a part of the Russian Church of North America grew steadily so that, on the eve of World War I, it had four bishoprics and three missions: the Albanian, the Syrian and the Serbian. Until the Revolution of 1917

---

[1]The problem of the Doukhobors, or Wrestlers with the Spirit, is confused by some sensational episodes reported in a still more sensational way by newspapers. Certainly their anarchism and communistic tendencies as well as their strange observances did not fit into Canadian life, but somehow the whole question was also mishandled by the authorities. Despite all the difficulties there is evidence that during some sixty years of their stay they adjusted themselves to the new environment, and there is a possibility that they will one day dissolve into Canadian Protestantism. For the time being they have already split into four groups: the Independents, who are almost completely assimilated; the Community members, who desire to conform to existing social norms; the Sharing Doukhobors, who have broken away from the Sons of Freedom and are trying to adapt themselves to their surroundings; and the Freedomites, the small remainder of the sect, who are on the verge of splitting again. So long as there is no source to feed the group with new energy, Canadian life will stimulate even the most stubborn Sons of God with their biblical illiteracy to begin to look for readjustment. Among the rich literature on the subject there is a very good and balanced account of the conflict between the sect and new conditions in a book by F. P. Zubek and P. A. Solberg entitled *Doukhobors at War* (Toronto, 1952).

the Russian Orthodox Church in America was controlled by an archbishop appointed by the Holy Synod in Russia and supported by an annual subsidy from the Tsar's treasury. Officially, it was a Russian church and its mission was not only to take care of the religious needs of the immigrants but still more to secure their loyalty to the Tsar. For that reason the Russian Orthodox Church in Canada did not try to adapt itself to its new surroundings. Except for some itinerant priests who went beyond their official duty and made sincere attempts to help some fellow-countrymen by giving them advice in organizing independent religious communities, the church did not seek to understand the real wants of the immigrants and was consequently distrusted by them.[1] Living in close bondage to the Russia of the Tsars, the Russian Orthodox Church on this continent later suffered all the consequences of the troubles of a Russia in distress without being able to benefit from the opportunities offered by a politically and religiously free society.

After the Bolshevik *coup d'état*, the church in Toronto was closed and its property sold. Some other Russian churches on the continent followed this example. After that the Russian Church remained disorganized for a long time. In February, 1919, a church council with the participation of laymen elected an archbishop and instituted an autonomous Russian Orthodox Church of North America. In 1925 a representative of the "Living Church" under the Bolshevik regime took over the Russian church in New York and other properties there, creating a "time of troubles" within the Russian Orthodox community over the whole North American continent. Another administrative split took place when the Russian *emigré* clergy in Yugoslavia constituted a "church council abroad" and elected another metropolitan who claimed that the Church of America belonged to his jurisdiction.

This dispute was not yet settled when a new disruption occurred within the Russian Church in Canada. Influenced by patriotic feelings revived among the Russians in America during World War II, and stirred by the appointment of a new patriarch in Moscow, the Council of the Russian Church decided by a majority of votes on September 12, 1946, that the Russian Orthodox Church of North

[1] J. Davis, *The Russian Immigrant* (New York, 1922), p. 91.

America considered itself to be under the jurisdiction of the Patriarch of Moscow. The partisans of the metropolitan elected by the Russian council in Yugoslavia refused to accept this decision and withdrew their churches from the main body. Several years later, some churches that had recognized the Patriarch of Moscow denied his authority over the Russian Church in America on account of his equivocal position under the Soviet government, but they did not want to join his former opponents in the Council. They are somewhat isolated today and their stand is not yet clearly defined.[1]

Thus the Russian Orthodox Church of North America, which had the prerequisites necessary for amalgamating all other Orthodox churches on this continent, failed to do so because of its inner tensions and divisions as well as of causes beyond its control.

V

From the point of view of adjustment to the new country, the experience of the Ukrainians in Canada is the most important and the most illuminating. The Ukrainians constitute the largest ethnic group among all the immigrants from eastern Europe, and their background is very complex. They came away from two different foreign dominations, Russian on the one hand and Austrian, later Polish, on the other, and they had already been divided for centuries between two churches of Eastern rites: Orthodox and Uniate. Last but not least, they brought along a tendency to separate themselves from other churches on nationalistic and religious grounds.

For the first time in their long history, the Ukrainians found themselves under a foreign rule with full political freedom and religious tolerance. They were given an opportunity to express their national sentiments and organize free religious communities. But their economic condition at the beginning, the somewhat perplexing religious arrangements in Canada and their own traditional attitudes worked towards creating a confusing situation. The Ukrainians were very slow in setting up congregations, despite a steady and strong influx of newcomers from their homeland that should have enabled

[1] L. I. Strakhovsky, "Istoricheskii obzor russkoi pravoslavnoi itserkvi v Sev. Amerike," *Iubileinyi Sbornik k 25-ia Khrame Khrista Spasitelia v g. Toronto 1930-1955* (New York, 1955), p. 20f.

them to establish a fast-growing church. Certainly, the old division between the Orthodox and the Uniates[1] was quite a serious obstacle, but even where a uniform settlement was achieved the Ukrainians continued to gather in private homes for worship. Two reasons explain their lack of initiative in building churches and securing priests of their own. In their old country the government had ordinarily erected churches and supplied priests. Furthermore, the Ukrainians were accustomed to praying at home in front of an icon, for where there is an icon there is room for prayers; regular church-going was not a universal practice. Under the impact of the prevailing *diaspora* spirit, Ukrainian immigrants enlarged their family worship, for which some of them had precedents in their native lands, and made it into a gathering for worship of all friends and neighbours in the community.

This situation became intolerable when the settlers had to go to the clergy of other churches for marriages, baptisms and burial services, and they began to ask for priests of their own persuasion. Their plea for religious help was answered by four different groups: the Russian Orthodox, the Roman Catholics, the Presbyterians and the Baptists. The most successful were the itinerant priests sent by the Russian Orthodox Church of North America and financed by the Tsarist government. They were popular because their rites corresponded to those with which the settlers were familiar, their fees were very small, and they advocated independent congregations free from the Russian Church. The last factor was of great importance, for the Ukrainian Orthodox were suspicious of Russian ecclesiastical administration, while the Uniates resented any attempt to incorporate them into the Roman Church.

But these itinerant priests were not able to satisfy the needs of the growing communities for ever. Metropolitan Seraphim's attempt to establish an All-Russian Orthodox Church in 1902 was therefore quite successful. He claimed to have been consecrated by the Patriarch of Constantinople, whom the Ukrainians had always recognized as their supreme authority; and he sought out ordained priests from among the settlers themselves, meeting in this way their desire for

[1]E. Winter, *Byzanz und Rom im Kampf um die Ukraine 955-1939* (Leipzig, 1942), p. 66f.

independence. At the beginning, Metropolitan Seraphim attracted about one-third of the whole Ukrainian population in Canada. But his spectacular success was soon clouded by the fact that he ordained without discrimination almost anyone who could read and pay the fee, and he later showed signs of insanity. Priests and laymen alike abandoned him, and in 1908 he was forced to leave for Russia, where he vanished.[1]

At the time of Metropolitan Seraphim's meteoric career a short-lived Independent Greek Church with Protestant leanings began to emerge from the All-Russian Orthodox Church. The Ukrainians' call for evangelical care had also been answered by the Presbyterian Church, and the origins of this new movement must be sought there. Towards the end of the nineteenth century, the Presbyterians were looking for Ukrainian young men who after special training could interpret the Canadian way of life to their compatriots. With this objective in view they enrolled Ivan Bodrug and some other Ukrainians at Manitoba College, teaching them English and some theology. Bodrug was interested in organizing an evangelical church similar to one he had known in Galicia. The Presbyterians urged him to accept Protestant ordination, but he considered it necessary to have a Ukrainian evangelical church founded by Ukrainians. When Metropolitan Seraphim appeared, Bodrug and some of his colleagues saw their opportunity and had themselves ordained by him. Then, in 1904, when the metropolitan was temporarily absent, Bodrug and fourteen other priests secured the financial support of the Presbyterian Church, separated from the All-Russian Orthodox Church, and constituted the Independent Greek Church. The Greek rites and ecclesiastical robes were retained, but otherwise the main tenets of Protestant Christian teaching were followed, and the church's consistory composed of all the priests and an equal number of laymen could not take any important step without the approval of the synodical Committee of Home Missions.

The development of the Independent Greek Church was so encouraging that the Presbyterian Church began to look upon itself as destined to shape the moral and intellectual life of the Ukrainians. It instructed the clergy of the Independent Greek Church to recom-

[1]P. Yuzyk, *The Ukrainians in Manitoba* (Toronto, 1953), p. 72.

mend to the Ukrainians some schools that were under its supervision, and in 1907 it ordered all Orthodox forms to be discarded. The Ukrainians reacted with a tremendous outcry against this attempt at assimilation and Anglicization. Some priests resigned, and many members of the church started to go to other churches. A controversy arose between Bodrug and another priest, Bychinsky. Bodrug was of the opinion that the Ukrainians were deeply rooted in Eastern Orthodox forms and would not accept the less colourful Protestant liturgy. He also thought it necessary that his church should officially remain independent from the Presbyterian Church. Bychinsky favoured closer ties with the Presbyterian Church, and his view was favoured by Presbyterian leaders. Bodrug left for the United States, and the Presbyterian Church formally absorbed the Independent Orthodox Church with twenty-seven priests, some of whom lost their entire congregations.[1]

This failure, according to Presbyterian authorities, was due to the lack of well-trained Ukrainian missionaries able to emphasize the positive message of Protestantism. Be that as it may, there was also a negative aspect that was not taken into consideration: the opposition of the Ukrainians to the old traditional churches, which had oppressed them at home and had made them suspicious of any church showing a tendency to absorb them. As one Presbyterian wrote, "The experiment was rather too complex for a great democratic body like the Presbyterian Church to handle."[2]

Baptist missionary work, a continuation of efforts in the Ukraine and in the United States, was supported and supervised by the Baptist Union. It was not on the same scale as that attempted by the Presbyterians, and it was no more successful. The basic reasons for failure were the same. In the case of the Baptists, however, internal struggles within a very weak community also contributed to schisms amont the Ukrainians; today three very small distinct Baptist churches exist side by side among the Ukrainians in Saskatoon.[3]

[1]M. Zuk, "The Ukrainian Protestant Missions," thesis in manuscript for Faculty of Divinity, McGill University, Montreal, 1957, p. 78.

[2]A. J. Hunter, *A Friendly Adventure: the Story of the United Church among New Canadians at Teulon, Manitoba* (Toronto, 1929), p. 34.

[3]W. C. Smalley, "Ukrainian Baptist Work through Fifty Years," *Canadian Baptist Home Missions Digest*, Vol. II (1955), p. 122.

After the disappearance of the Independent Greek Church the majority of the Ukrainians belonged to two violently opposed religious groups, the Russian Orthodox and the Greek Catholic. At home the Ukrainian Greek Catholics, or Uniates, were united in the Ruthenian Greek Catholic Church. This church had come into existence in eastern Europe in 1596 when some of the Orthodox bishops recognized the supremacy of the pope in Rome but retained their Eastern rites and the use of Old Slavonic in their liturgy. In Canada the Uniates had to fight for their identity against the attempts of the Roman clergy to annex them to Roman Catholic dioceses. They began to defect to the Russian Orthodox and the Independent Greek Churches. On account of these defections, they were at last given a Ukrainian bishop, Budka.

In 1913 the Greek Catholic Church was incorporated, removed from the jurisdiction of the Roman Catholic Church in Canada and made directly responsible to the pope who nominates the bishops. Thus the foundation for a prosperous future was laid. The fact that Greek Catholic priests could now appeal to Ukrainian nationalism naturally weakened the hold of the Russian Orthodox Church and offered favourable prospects for absorbing not only the Uniates but also the Ukrainian Orthodox. Very soon, however, Bishop Budka estranged a part of the Ukrainian Catholic intelligentsia by trying to introduce Latin into the Greek Catholic liturgy. He also stirred up Ukrainian nationalistic feelings by issuing a pastoral letter urging his parishioners to return to their homeland and fight for Austria. Ever since this appeal the Ukrainian Greek Catholic Church has been decreasing in numbers, and not even the change of designation from Ruthenian to Ukrainian in 1951 could stem the tide.[1]

During the Russian Revolution of 1917 the Ukrainians saw in the breakdown of the Tsarist regime the end of their national suffering and made an ardent effort to establish a sovereign state of their own. This event at home gave rise to an astounding nationalism among the Ukrainians in Canada and created an atmosphere in which there was not much room for either the Russian or the Ruthenian churches to manoeuvre. Both were alien by name, and both represented vestiges

[1]C. H. Young, *op. cit.*, p. 134f.

of former foreign domination. As a consequence of this nationalistic enthusiasm the Ukrainian Greek Orthodox Church was founded on the initiative of some intellectuals in 1918. This church was joined at once by a great number of Orthodox as well as Greek Catholics, and it has continued to attract more and more Ukrainians ever since.[1]

Remembering the bitter experience in the past, the Sobor (an assembly of the clergy and delegates of the brotherhoods and congregations) laid down a number of fundamental principles by which the newly organized church was to be guided. The new church accepted the same dogmas and the same rites as other Eastern Orthodox churches. All priests had to be married. All the bishops were to be elected by the Sobor. The church congregation was to own all property and to have jurisdiction over it. The Sobor was somewhat vague in determining relations with churches, although it decided that the church was to be in communion with other Orthodox churches. There was a general opinion that the new church had to be connected with the home church. In 1919 the church recognized the primacy of the Patriarch of Antioch, not that of the Patriarch of Constantinople, but it continued to regard itself as part of the church in the Ukraine until it became fully independent.

In the thirties a great controversy on the question of the relationship to the home church flared up and threatened to disrupt the Ukrainian church in Canada. The problem was finally solved in 1948, when the Ukrainian Greek Orthodox Church of Canada was proclaimed autocephalous. That same year Metropolitan Ilarion, formerly of the autocephalous Orthodox Church of Poland, was brought to Canada by the Cathedral congregation of St. Mary in Winnipeg, which had become independent while the controversy was at its peak. The metropolitan headed this church until 1951, when the Sobor elected him also the head of the Ukrainian Greek Orthodox Church of all Canada. In this way the Ukrainian Orthodox churches were reunited, and the first Canadian territorial Orthodox church was firmly established. The main bond of the new church is ethnic rather than territorial, however, the term "Ukrainian" differentiating it from other Slavonic Orthodox congregations.

[1]P. Yuzyk, *op. cit.*, p. 76f.

At the moment, the Serbian Orthodox Church is passing through a serious crisis that threatens to disrupt its unity. The Serbian Orthodox appeared in Canada as a few churches with small congregations. They remained under the jurisdiction of the Russian Orthodox Church of North America until 1923, when a Serbian Orthodox diocese for the United States and Canada with its see at Libertywill was established. At its head is a bishop who is under the jurisdiction of the patriarch in Yugoslavia. Because of the political situation in Yugoslavia, some of the clergy think that the patriarch is under the control of the government and that the Serbian Orthodox Church on the continent should become autocephalous; others are against this separation. The Serbian laymen are also divided.

The remaining Orthodox believers—Greek, Rumanian, Armenian, Georgian and Albanian—have not had such a turbulent past and, except for the Rumanian congregations consisting mainly of Slavonic Bukovinians, have largely been isolated by language barriers from other Eastern Christian communities in Canada. Most of their religious communities have been handicapped by the smallness of their membership but have struggled for years to organize congregations and to build and maintain churches.

These conditions have caused many serious worries for Orthodox Christians in Canada, and the idea of amalgamating several Orthodox churches emerged some years ago. It is still cherished today by some representatives of the Eastern Churches, though for the time being it has to remain an ideal. The situation was summed up correctly by one outstanding representative who said, "It would be too difficult yet for the several churches to give up their strong nationalistic and individualistic character and merge all the elements into one homogeneous group."[1]

VI

The impact of the new country could not erase the strongly nationalistic and individualistic character of the churches to which the different ethnic groups belong. On the contrary, conditions in Canada seem to encourage these tendencies, at least in the first generation of

[1] P. Yuzyk, in *Encyclopedia Canadiana*, Vol. 8, p. 66.

newcomers, and the memory of past historical events in Europe does not favour assimilation. Linguistic obstacles not only confuse cultural patterns but provoke feelings of anxiety among immigrants, who are forced to seek security in getting together with people of the same tongue and the same background. The North American tradition of highly organized church life, especially in such fields as Christian education and community life, also fosters this tendency to stay together. The Sunday School and the social gatherings of the congregation promote the preservation of the native vernacular and old-country attitudes; they satisfy the gregarious needs of the ethnic group and develop a spirit of *diaspora*. The real problem of religious adjustment lies with the first generation born in Canada, a generation that begins to question and negate the purpose and value of such a secluded circle. These young people are torn between their family background and their education in Canadian schools in another language, which almost without exception becomes their only means of expressing themselves adequately. In their split-personality existence they turn against their parents' religious community and grow weary in their efforts to be absorbed into Canadian society. A consequence of their inner struggle is that some are breaking away from their old religious group. They either stay aloof from any religious group or, under the influence of their closest Canadian surroundings, join a traditional church, usually one that has some resemblance to their former church. Others, however, stay with the religious community of their parents. They either display only slight interest in congregational activities or slowly readjust themselves to the Orthodox view of life with the help of understanding parents or—more likely—of well-educated and tolerant priests.

From generation to generation the process of readjustment continues. As long as the native vernaculars are kept as the means of communication within the congregations, and as long as the national frame of mind is systematically nursed, cultural and religious conflicts will persist. Without a common language for divine service the prospects are very small for more intimate co-operation among the Orthodox churches in Canada, consequently for the ultimate formation of a territorial Canadian Orthodox Church.

There is a further problem of no slight significance. Centralized church organizations on a strongly ethnic basis belong to Orthodox tradition. They even endeavour to embrace those members of the ethnic group that are living outside the national boundaries. It is true that under the influence of the Canadian scene, with its voluntary religious communities, the Orthodox immigrants had to set up self-supporting congregations. This made them, in a sense, independent from their central church bodies, but their independence is normally limited to certain practices such as the right of the community to discuss the acceptance of one priest or another with the higher ecclesiastical authority. That this tradition of an all-embracing national church is very strong can be shown by the examples of the Russian and Serbian Orthodox churches in the United States and Canada. These have not yet been able to decide definitely in which form they will assert their autonomy in relation to their mother churches, although they both have a very plausible reason for separation—Communist control of the mother churches!

The question of Canadian influence may be posed in the case of the Ukrainian Greek Orthodox Church because of its democratic character, which is demonstrated by the role of the laity in deciding the policies of the church and in electing its bishops. But it is essentially a national Ukrainian church, and it was founded and declared independent for national reasons—to distinguish itself from Roman Catholicism as well as from Protestantism, to free itself from possible interference by the Communist government in Russia through the home church, and to preserve the ethnic unity of the Ukrainians in Canada. Whatever the reasons may be, this church represents the first and only adaptation to the Canadian pattern by organizing a territorial church within the boundaries of Canada. A further step in the same direction cannot be expected as long as newly elated nationalism has not lived its full life.

The ideological rift between the Communist world and ours, especially with respect to the treatment of religion and church, may eventually lead to the separation of certain Orthodox churches from their mother churches. If the Canadian Orthodox churches do not develop a strong Canadianism, however, Orthodox churches in North America will tend towards organization along ethnic lines with their central authorities in the United States.

As may be seen from this survey, the main obstacle to co-operation has been a habit of thinking in terms of institutionalism with all the accompanying problems of language barriers, old-country customs and historical prejudices. Support was readily given to needy congregations by other churches in the best Christian spirit. It was not necessary, many Canadian Orthodox noted, to have a united organization as *conditio sine qua non* in order to make a Christian community help Christians of another church. In the same spirit the Christian churches can face the challenge of our changing society. The past experience of Orthodox churches should serve as guidance for wider and more intimate co-operation to meet the needs of mankind without waiting to clear the terrain for unified institutional organization.

10

SECTARIAN TRADITION IN CANADA
JOHN S. MOIR

In Canada sects have been almost exclusively of Protestant origin, although sectarianism is not a distinctively Protestant or even Christian phenomenon. Every religious movement, as soon as it begins to adapt or accommodate to its terrestrial environment, tends to produce its own sectarian echo. The aim of the sect is to restore the original purity of the true faith by returning to the source of the movement, ignoring and rejecting all that has happened in the meantime, namely the accumulation of tradition.

But if tradition is the memory and conscience of the church, does a sectarian tradition also exist in Canada? Is there a distinguishable *Canadian* sectarian tradition? Any answers to these questions cannot hope to receive complete acceptance, if for no other reason than that even scholars do not agree as to what constitutes a sect.

From the point of view of the sects, and of the law, sects do not exist. However small or large, however inconsequential or important, however pagan or Christian, all religious groupings seem to be incorporated as churches. Nevertheless, the sect can be differentiated from both church and cult by several criteria.[1]

A "sect" can be defined as a body of persons agreed upon religious doctrines usually different from those of an established or orthodox church from which they have separated and usually having distinctive common worship. But the inclusion of "usually" limits the utility of this definition, and the reference to doctrinal differences opens vast areas for discussion. A second definition, "a nonconformist or other

[1]The term "denomination," used in the United States specifically to describe a church-structured organization within a political state where no form of establishment exists, has in Canada a much looser but more literal usage, being applied to any autonomous religious body, whether church- or sect-structured, which can be distinguished by name.

church as described by opponents," begs the question of the relation of sect to church, but does point up the common pejorative use of the word. Another definition, "a religious denomination," is too generalized to be useful, but the description, "a party or faction in a religious body," does provide a base for this inquiry since it preserves the sense of the Latin root *secta*—a faction or following, with connotations of separation, distinction and protest. The common definition of "church" as "an organized Christian society at any time" would cover the sect too, but it reminds us that we are concerned only with Christian sects and justifies the exclusion of several groups that pass for sects in common parlance.

"Sect," then, involves division, protest and separation, and popularly implies smallness of numbers. The North American sect is fundamentalist, evangelistic, Bible-centred and traditionally anti-traditionalist in its emphasis. It stresses the necessity for conversion as a condition of membership, a fact which leads Richard Niebuhr to say that the true sect exists for only one generation.[1] The sect is totalitarian in its demand for strict behavioural conformity, and like the totalitarian state is aggressively militant in its symbolism and defensive in its outlook. It requires total obedience and loyalty, opposing membership in other organizations as contaminating. The sect stresses proselytization, particularly through overseas missions, and it affords a larger role to women in its democratic, congregationally autonomous organization. It combats worldliness in all its aspects—dress, amusements and possessions—reminding its members of the imminent needle's eye. The sect is anticlerical, anti-intellectual as shown by its reliance on a God-ordained ministry, anti-scientific especially in its response to the theory of evolution, and anti-state in its disregard for national boundaries and, at times, for national laws. To these factors the sociologist adds more general characteristics. The sect is "the church of the disinherited," of the economically inferior and socially uprooted. Hence the sectarian will be found most frequently in the lower class, less often in the middle class. Movement from the former socio-economic group to the other should normally be accompanied by transfer from sect to church in the case of the individual or mutation of sect into church if the bulk

[1] *The Social Sources of Denominationalism* (New York: Meridian Books, 1957), p. 19.

of the sect membership is involved in the change of status. Today, however, "disinheritance" is frequently social rather than economic. The sect member driving a Cadillac or power-boat reflects the disparity between Canadian class structure and income level.

Obviously the sum of these characteristics will rarely if ever be found in one sect. Nevertheless the sect is clearly distinguishable from the church. The church is bureaucratic in organization, either individually or corporately hierarchically structured, accommodated to society, latitudinarian in ideology—it accepts different ethical standards for different social classes—and more or less traditionalist by comparison with the sect. But between the abstracted church and the idealized sect lies a spectrum of churchy sects and sectarian churches. Sects become respectable by accommodation as expensive buildings and more worldly behaviour reflect the economic success of members. In many churches evidence of sectarian influence can be discovered, whether inherited from previous sect status or acquired by adaptation to local conditions.

On the North American continent, which early provided a refuge for European sects, sectarianism has found particularly fertile soil for its ideals and techniques. Historically the sects have been numerous on this continent, although their individual membership has encompassed only a very small proportion of the total population. Despite paucity of membership, the sects have frequently exerted a disproportionately large influence on social and political developments. E. T. Clark[1] has grouped American sects into seven categories which deserve attention as they apply to Canadian sectarianism. The "pessimistic" sects include the Millerites and their successors, the Seventh-Day Adventists and the Jehovah's Witnesses, though the last-named can be ignored on the grounds that it has departed from Christian doctrine. The next group, "perfectionist" sects, includes historically the Methodists and their ideological offspring such as the Holiness Movement and the Church of the Nazarene. Of the hundred-odd sects in the United States, about one-half grew out of Methodism. By the mid-nineteenth century the Wesleyan Methodist churches in North America—to distinguish them from the small Methodist sects—had progressed from sect to church, a process

[1] E. T. Clark, *The Small Sects in America* (Nashville, 1927), pp. 26-29.

which Wesley himself had foreseen when he wrote, "The Methodists in every place grow diligent and frugal; consequently they increase in goods."[1] The next category comprises the "legalistic" sects who claim to be sole heirs to the true and early church, and who by such practices as foot-washing and plain dressing stress the primitiveness of their Christianity. The sects noted as legalistic—for example the Reformed Episcopal and Primitive Baptist—have had no significant place in Canadian church history. Similarly, such "charismatic" sects as the Church of God and the "holy rollers" who stress tongues and prophecy have made no noticeable contribution to any sectarian tradition in this country if for no other reason than that "perfectionist" sects have accepted such phenomena as part of their own sectarian tradition.

With "communistic" sects it is more difficult to deal in a Canadian context. Hutterites and Doukhobors have an important place in our collective national religious life, more so than in the United States melting pot. Here is the ultimate in the rejection of accommodation, yet the same form of withdrawal can be seen in early Mennonite and Lutheran communities in eastern Canada. Perhaps a clue lies in the broader field of cultural rather than religious separation. Canadian communistic groups are invariably of non-English, non-French extraction, and preservation of their language is a large part of their motivation. If such groups are sects, the language barrier has prevented them from contributing to any general Canadian sectarian tradition, but they may be treated more conveniently as a separate church tradition outside the scope of this study. Finally, two sect-types that can be dismissed as being either non-Christian or non-sect are the scientific, hedonistic "egocentric" groups such as the Christian Science Church or "The Great I Am," which are best defined as cults, and the mystic, occult "esoteric" groups such as Baha'i and the Rosicrucians, which are not even Christian.

In the two centuries since the bulk of present-day Canada came under British sovereignty, at least three distinct periods of sectarian activity can be distinguished: the first in the Great Awakening of the Newlight movement; the second in the Great Revival in Upper Canada; and the last beginning contemporaneously—and not

[1] *Works of the Rev. John Wesley* (New York: Carlton and Porter, 3rd American edition), VII, 317.

coincidentally—with Confederation, with the first church unions, with intensive industrialization and urbanization in central Canada, and with the opening of the West. In each of these periods sectarianism was a reaction or protest against different things: in the first period against the political involvement of the New England establishment, in the second against the Erastian privileges of the Anglican establishment in Upper Canada, and in the third against the latitudinarianism, social respectability and service-club "togetherness" of the modern conventionalized churches.

Canada is the product of two counter-revolutions. The Counter-Reformation stamped New France with that religious zeal and piety which gives French Canada its distinctive character to this day, while British reaction to the American Revolution ensured that the Second Empire in North America would differ markedly from the American republic to the south. These counter-revolutionary traditions have worked against the growth of sectarianism in Canada—the French tradition by its exclusivism and ultramontanism, the British by its equation of religious dissent with republicanism and treason. Thanks to the Counter-Reformation, the province of Quebec neither produced nor shared in any sectarian tradition.

Nova Scotia had been British for almost half a century before a change in Imperial policy introduced the elements in which the Newlight movement was to grow. The so-called "Charter of Nova Scotia," issued in 1759 to encourage settlement, attracted enough immigrants from New England to make the colony a projection in time and space of New England. The promise of religious freedom for Protestant dissenters was not the least of the attractions. New England Puritanism had but recently lost the sectarian characteristic of accepting members by conversion only, a characteristic which had produced in those colonies an oligarchic theocracy with little room for dissenters. This immigration to Nova Scotia was ended after a decade by the opening of the Ohio Valley with all the opportunity and freedom from institutional limitations that accompany a new frontier.

In New England, Puritanism was rapidly accommodating itself to a society of the remaining "half-saved" when the Great Awakening reached Nova Scotia in 1775. This date in itself might suggest some connection with the political events of the Revolution. All the evidence is to the contrary, however, for the Great Awakening, which had begun with Whitefield in the colonies to the south, swept into Nova Scotia apparently in total disregard of political considerations. Indeed, the Great Awakening in Nova Scotia seemed to profit by the Revolution, for it fed on an accommodated Nova Scotian Congregationalism that was too sympathetic to rebellion.

The Newlight movement offered the neutral Yankees of Nova Scotia a religious solution to their political neutrality. Henry Alline had found his own escape from chill Calvinism in personal conversion in 1775. His charismatic qualities and the sectarian nature of the Newlight provided a catalyst for elements of religious dissatisfaction already present in the colony. As a sectarian movement the Newlight cut across established denominational lines; its divisive effects were soon condemned by Anglicans, Presbyterians, Methodists and even some Congregationalists. Here was the first Canadian encounter between British ecclesiasticism and the inherent sectarianism of the New World with its frontier conditions. Loyalists arriving in Nova Scotia brought with them or soon absorbed the Newlight, which in turn they spread as they opened new frontiers of settlement in the colony. Despite Alline's death in 1784 the Newlight movement continued to spread in Nova Scotia—to the distress of such as Bishop Inglis, who in 1799 was complaining of these "enthusiasts." But this first great North American sectarian movement had run its course in Nova Scotia by 1810. Its close alliance with Baptists, stemming from their common Calvinism, ended in the absorption of the Newlight into the Baptist churches, a victory for ecclesiasticism in spite of the inherent sectarian tendencies of the Baptists. But the element of Calvinism in the Newlight movement was unusual if not unique, and certainly was a distinctive ingredient of Canadian sectarianism.

Whereas the Newlight movement had succeeded in Nova Scotia because it was accepted as a political neutral (which Congregationalism was not), the Great Revival in Upper Canada was from the outset identified rightly or wrongly with the American Revolution. Perhaps it was the presence of British influence in the person of military forces and government functionaries that made Bishop Inglis less critical of the Newlight movement than were his colleagues in the Canadas or its counterpart there. After the dimming of the Newlight, the people of Nova Scotia, sects included, tended to look eastward for inspiration, to receive a distinctly European outlook which thereafter put a quietus on sectarian agitation by accommodating sectarianism to Erastian tradition. In Upper Canada, however, official criticism of sectarians began at a time when it might have been least expected.

Methodist influences in the colony had been from the outset of American origin. Though early and spontaneous classes had been organized among the Loyalists, the sect owed its organization in Upper Canada to Nathan Bangs and other American Methodists of the Genesee Conference. Imperial authorities had professed to find a causal relation between sectarianism and revolution in the Thirteen Colonies, and to ensure the loyalty of the truncated Second Empire in North America gave the Church of England a preferred position if not a full establishment. Imperial policy was intended to establish in North America, albeit belatedly, the European principle of *cuius regio eius religio*, which had been transplanted so successfully a century before in New France. In the two Canadas, British policy included the reservation of one-seventh of the surveyed land for the profit of the "Protestant" clergy. It therefore seems strange that there had been no official objection to American Methodist infiltration during the War of 1812 or immediately afterwards when legislative action severly restricted the legal position of American citizens in the province. Anti-American pressure was, however, felt strongly within the Canadian Methodist body; it led to the move in 1824 by the Canadians for complete separation from the Genesee Conference, a move completed in 1828 by the establishment of an autonomous Canadian Methodist organization. But no open attack on sectarianism was made until 1826 when Archdeacon Strachan's funeral sermon for the late Bishop Mountain was published.

Two explanations may be offered for this sudden official interest in sectarian growth. In the first place, the hegemony of the Church of England had already been challenged by the Church of Scotland's claim to co-establishment in the Empire and a share of the Clergy Reserves. This was a direct threat to the Anglican monopoly, but it did not involve sectarianism. The second explanation may lie in the vast numerical increase of Methodism. Its use of itinerant preachers and revivalistic camp meetings was rapidly winning a frontier population from the sedentary churches by default. In Prince Edward

County, for instance, its organizational advantages enabled it to take over the highly decentralized and incohesive Quaker groups. It has been estimated that in the mid-twenties perhaps more than a half of the colony's population were attached to the Methodists. Thus it may have been simply the challenge of numbers from the sects that prompted Strachan's outburst. No such problem faced his bishop in Lower Canada.

The publication of Strachan's charges—that the Methodist preachers were uneducated, unsettled, politically minded and American (hence anti-monarchical) and hostile to "the parent Church"—provoked a reply from the young Egerton Ryerson defending some of the main sectarian characteristics.[1] The Methodist preachers are God-inspired men preaching the gospel without government subsidies; and education is acquired in other ways and other places than colleges. Seven-eighths of the Methodist teachers are British born, and of the rest all but two are naturalized citizens. They are serving God, not Mammon—it is Strachan who is politically minded! At least Bishop Stewart recognized that this opposition was not directed against Anglicanism but against that church-state relationship which gave the Church of England "the character of an establishment."[2]

The argument was destined to assume a political tone that would mark out the boundary of sectarian tradition for coming generations. Strachan had said that a Christian nation without an establishment is a contradiction, and around the issue of establishment *versus* voluntarism the basic *Canadian* sectarian tradition grew up. On the one side were the churches, particularly the Anglican, equating religious protest with political disloyalty in the best Royalist and tory tradition. Opposed were the dissenters upholding what had become a New World tradition in itself, the separation of church and state. The fact that separation was embodied in the First Amendment to the Constitution of the United States was, understandably, not cited by sectarians already smarting from the accusation of republicanism! But in any case the accusation was largely groundless, as

[1]A. E. Ryerson, *Canadian Methodism: its Epochs and Characteristics* (Toronto, 1882), pp. 140-160.
[2]T. R. Millman, *The Life of the Right Reverend, the Honourable Charles James Stewart* (London, Ont., 1953), pp. 72-73.

the sectarians had proven in the American Revolution and in 1812, and were to prove again in 1837. The six Ryerson brothers, five of whom were Methodist teachers, could claim the title of U.E.L. as Strachan could not. Upper Canadian sectarians of the colonial period were in the awkward position of holding two contrary traditions—those of the British and loyalist counter-revolution and the North American voluntarist revolution. The established, co-established and semi-established churches of England, Scotland and Rome were virtually unencumbered by North American influences.

During the next quarter century the churches held firmly to vestigial remains of establishment, but one by one such rights (or were they privileges?) as the monopoly of marriages and church burials, direct political representation in the legislative councils, control of the educational system, and enjoyment of the Clergy Reserves and Rectory lands, were swept into the limbo of undenominational nationalization or—equally obnoxious—shared with the sectarians. As late as 1841 membership in the Legislative Council of Canada was divided equally between the three churches, but three years later the Methodists could boast that the appointment of Ryerson as Superintendent of Education gave them their first public office. Strachan might charge that to infringe the Anglican university endowment monopoly was to equate Christian truth with sectarian error,[1] but the forces of sectarianism seemed irresistible. New strength to the sectarian cause came with the Disruption of the Kirk. Now, remarked one anticlerical Presbyterian, the followers of Knox would have a choice of religion other than St. Giles or Canterbury.[2]

But the growth of sectarianism in the province—the appearance of the voluntarist Free Church, the Methodist New Connexion, and other groups—was in fact transforming the Wesleyan Methodists into a church. The old Methodists were accommodating themselves to the new order of possession as their church acquired physical structures and their members wealth. The torch of voluntarism passed to the other sectarian groups when their Methodist college took government money and when the Methodist Church shared in

[1] J. G. Hodgins, *Documentary History of Education in Upper Canada* (Toronto, 1894-1910), V, 27.
[2] Isaac Buchanan to William Morris, July 5, 1844. Morris Papers, Queen's University Library.

the spoils of the Clergy Reserves. The turning point for sect and church was reached soon after mid-century. Officially no establishment remained and the Canadian sectarian tradition had lost its *raison d'être*.

For the Churches of England and Scotland the loss of status was a blessing in disguise. True, they would continue to preserve their trans-Atlantic orientation, though in an ever-diminishing degree, but the way was now open to the forces of indigenization. The Church of England in Canada soon received self-government and set a pattern for church organization in the rest of the Empire. The Church of Scotland soon acquired its first native-born minister. The only aspect of sectarianism in Canada that was distinctively Canadian seemed to pass into the realm of tradition. But tradition is a persistent thing. The rectories still exist in law and fact. The Church of England stands first on the ladder of precedence, with the Church of Rome on the next rung also occupying its peculiar position in the province of Quebec. United Church buildings are still referred to by some as "meeting houses," and conservatives have discovered a close relationship between the United Church and the political left. On the occasion of royal visits the suggestion is heard that the religiously divisible Crown should patronize the almost-national church!

In the generation between the secularization of the Clergy Reserves and the Methodist and Presbyterian unions, British North America achieved political unity, and Darwin produced a crisis in the course of the scientific revolution. The arrival of the railways and telegraphs, the founding of industrial enterprises, the growth of metropolitan centres—all these and other forces changed the very fabric of Canadian society. Within religious organizations the centralizing tendencies were obvious and reflected the disappearance of the frontier that had bred sectarianism. But the move from sect to church was not to go unchallenged. A new phase of sectarianism, the modern phase in Canada's history, began at this juncture in reaction against those very changes in religious, social and economic organization. As was the case in the Great Awakening which brought Newlightism to Nova Scotia, the modern period of sectarianism in Canada is North American, rather than Canadian, in origin. Such sectarian movements as have begun in Canada in the last century parallel similar movements in the United States. They must be considered as similar reactions to similar conditions, and they have been deeply influenced by and closely connected to their American counterparts. The sole exceptions to this North Americanism are the Salvation Army, which reached Canada from Britain eighty years ago; and the Plymouth Brethren, a "come-out" sect of the Church of Ireland, which arrived a few years earlier.

Like the Great Awakening, the Holiness Movement which appeared in the United States in the 1850's was at first inter-denominational and professed no desire to establish yet another "come-out" sect. Two generations earlier, certain "Scotch Baptists" in British North America had started a similar movement towards apostolic Christianity and Christian unity which ended in the separate existence of the Disciples of Christ. Now the expulsion of the "holy" nucleus from the Methodist Episcopals for criticizing the "easy, indulgent, accommodating, mammonized" church[1] created the seemingly inevitable sectarian structure—a new "church." It was no accident that the Free Methodists should arrive in Canada in 1876, just two years after the major Canadian Methodist churches had merged in an organic union. In their move to regain initial principles, to restore the sectarian tradition of "old-time religion" with its non-material status symbols, the Free Methodists drew their support from the "more disinherited" of the union, the "common folk," the rural poor. For this economic group, the unskilled or semi-skilled, there was even a special beatitude—"Blessed are the horny hands of toil." At the same time and for the same reasons the Mennonite Church was split by the sectarian force that created the United Missionary Church.

But one more factor must be credited with creating the sectarian revival—the new frontier in the West. Here the religious conditions of the East a half century earlier were re-created, and the modern phase of sectarianism in Canada remains to this day more obviously and intimately connected with the agrarian West than with the settled and industrialized East. Thus at the end of the First World War over 100 sects were noted in the Canadian West.[2] Of 480

[1] T. L. Smith, *Called Unto Holiness. The Story of the Nazarenes: the formative years* (Kansas City, [1962]), p. 29.
[2] W. G. Smith, *Building the Canadian Nation* ([Toronto], 1922), p. 162.

Pentecostal Assembly congregations, 415 are west of the Niagara Peninsula. Similarly, the Christian and Missionary Alliance and the Church of the Nazarene draw their greatest strength in Canada from the western provinces.

Two aspects of sectarianism in the Prairies deserve special attention, for they support the contentions that sects attract the disinherited and that they are international rather than territorialized. In the first place, the sects have had great success among foreign-born people—more than ten percent of all the Pentecostal Assemblies in Canada are non-English-speaking. Secondly, all of the sects operating in the Prairies have close connections with the neighbouring states to the south and several have their headquarters in the American Mid-West.

It is noteworthy that the Holiness Movement made no impression on the Maritime Provinces, where no significant sectarianism or sectarian tradition has appeared since the death of Alline's influence. But the Holiness Movement did lead to a belated sectarian development in Ontario about the turn of the century. The expulsion of the charismatic R. C. Horner from the Methodist Church because of his highly emotional evangelical campaigns resulted in 1895 in the establishment of the "Wesleyan Connection." This movement reversed the usual historical process by expanding into the Eastern United States. Internal sectarianism within the Wesleyan Connection in turn produced in 1916 the Standard Church, a body whose influence is largely confined to Ontario. The only other sectarian bodies that have failed to gain a foothold on the Canadian prairies are the "legalistic" Reformed Episcopal Church, which has only six congregations in the whole country, and the Calvinistic, millenarian, subsected Plymouth Brethren, whose 6,500 adherents are concentrated predominantly in Ontario and British Columbia.

Paradoxically, the Prairies which have been the hotbed of this modern phase of sectarianism also provided the *force majeure* of the church union of 1925. In Alberta the Great Depression and to some extent church union intensified sectarian activity. At the same time the Depression produced the Social Credit Party. This has led Canadian scholars to suggest that the sects of Alberta are the Social Credit party at a prayer meeting. If there was any truth in this proposition a generation ago, it seems untenable today when eighty-five percent of the province's population belong to seven denominations that cannot conceivably be called sects, and when thirty-five percent of the population are city dwellers. Nevertheless, the Social Credit party draws heavily on the sects for party leadership material and on sectarian attitudes within the larger churches for political support on the hustings. If the Prairie sects, so weak in numbers, have not produced a new type of theocracy in Alberta, at least they have developed forms of intersectarian co-operation in the exchange of preachers, combined promotion of evangelical rallies and joint support for the Youth for Christ Movement and similar organizations. Undoubtedly the explanation of the strength of Social Credit in Alberta and British Columbia is to be found not solely in the sects but in sectarian attitudes shared by members of the larger churches. The appeal of Social Credit to such persons is reminiscent of the religion-based political conservatism of early Victorian Canadian Methodism, when support for Christian measures and Christian men, in that order, was advocated to replace partisan politics. Revivalistic spirit and techniques have a prominent place in Social Credit gatherings, but then a less blatant non-denominational Christian religiosity is readily discernible in Canadian politics generally.

Is there a sectarian tradition in Canada? The answer must be in the affirmative, but with the qualification that in its broadest aspects the tradition is more properly described as North American. It is the tradition of the sect on the frontier—perfectionist and, excepting the strong Calvinist overtones of Alline's Newlightism, drawing most of its ideology and practices from the Methodist heritage. "Legalistic" sects have had little appeal to Canadians, probably because such sects are more traditional than emotional. "Pessimistic" sects have not held any early gains made, for hope deferred maketh the adventist sick. "Charismatic" sects have tended to be absorbed into "perfectionist" sects, for charisma is but one proof of holiness. Since the "communistic" sects in Canada —if they are sects—have not communicated any tradition, there remains only one vital North American sectarian tradition in Canada—the tradition of the "perfectionist" sects, drawn either from the Arminianism of the Methodists or the Calvinism of the Baptists. But the sects in Canada have never been so numerous or the membership so large as in the United States. The sectarian tradition in Canada repeats the old dictum about "Canada, the double negative"—not American, not British, but a peculiar amalgam of both. North American sectarianism and British ecclesiasticism have been mutually circumscribing within Canada.

Is there also a sectarian tradition that is peculiarly Canadian? Here the answer is undoubtedly affirmative. What H. H. Walsh has described as the projection of the church-sect controversy into the form of the church-state controversy[1] is peculiarly Canadian. This sectarian tradition could not exist in the United States, and in England it had died with the Puritan Commonwealth. Anti-establishmentarianism seems to be the only sectarian tradition which has a national foundation in this country. Canada, to paraphrase one Canadian sociologist, has preserved churchism to preserve itself.[2] Whenever military, economic, political or cultural absorption by the United States threatened, as in 1776, 1812, 1837, 1911 or even 1957, Canada has turned to its counter-revolutionary tradition for inspiration. And ecclesiasticism is a traditional part of that tradition. The sect serves the function of providing a counter weight to the over-centralizing tendencies of ecclesiasticism. In Canada this function has been moulded into a Canadian sectarian tradition of religious egalitarianism in a semi-Erastian state.

[1]"Church History", *Encyclopedia Canadiana* (Ottawa, 1957-8), II, 375.
[2]S. D. Clark, "The Religious Sect in Canadian Economic Development," in E. R. Blishen *et al.*, *Canadian Society* (Toronto, 1961), p. 386.

11

BLENDING TRADITIONS:
THE UNITED CHURCH OF CANADA

JOHN WEBSTER GRANT

The United Church of Canada is commonly regarded as an untraditional denomination. Those who framed its Basis of Union did their work at a time when new philosophies of religion were all the rage and when energies were being devoted to new methods of attack upon moral and social problems. Since union there has not been much time to evolve a new United Church tradition, and the revolutionary temper of our era has not encouraged the search for one. Many would dismiss a study of tradition in The United Church of Canada as a waste of effort.

Upon reflection, however, one realizes that the very existence of The United Church of Canada raises a number of important questions about tradition. Those who propose to unite churches must, consciously or unconsciously, take up positions in relation to the traditions they have inherited. Every decision they make will reflect their attitudes to tradition. And once the union has been consummated, the resulting church will betray its assumptions about tradition in the ways it transacts its business and speaks to its situation. One can read many documents relating to the history of the United Church before and after union without coming upon overt references to tradition. With a little alertness, however, one will find many clues indicating whether in the minds of its founders and members the United Church is a new church, a combination of several old churches, or something else again.

A study of tradition in The United Church of Canada naturally breaks chronologically into two sections: the terms in which the united church was conceived by its promoters and founders, and the attitudes and actions of those who have lived within its fellowship. The United Church was actively in formation for approximately twenty years; thirty-eight have elapsed since union. That is not many years in all, but enough to make possible a few conclusions.

The project of church union took shape during a period when traditional ways had little prestige. During the first decade of this century many writers were predicting that dogmatic theology would yield its place to sociology and the comparative study of religions. The social gospel was the excitement of the hour, and in Canada the church was preoccupied with the task of evangelizing new cities and a new west largely peopled by settlers from abroad. Impressed with the urgency of planning for the future, Christians had little regard for ecclesiastical heirlooms. They were looking for ideas and methods that would work.

To such a pragmatic generation the appeal of church union was inevitably in its novelty rather than in its promise of a rediscovery of forgotten riches. In the west and north, where impatient laymen were anticipating union in wholesale local amalgamations, disgust with the divisiveness of old traditions was almost universal. Antipathy to tradition became there a part of the accepted mystique of union. In less extreme forms it was a part of the national character. The Very Reverend George Pidgeon wrote in explanation of the United Church mind:

Devoted missionaries brought the Gospel message to the pioneers in the Canadian forest, and they brought it in the denominational forms in which they had received it. Undoubtedly they expected to establish here the same institutions that had mediated the divine Spirit to them at home, and to see it repeat its former success. But you cannot transfer the spirit, the atmosphere and the distinctive character of a religious community from one land to another. You may plant the seed in the new soil, but the old form will break up whenever the new life germinates. The men who brought the message became different in the new environment; the men with whom they associated and toiled were different; the product of their joint effort must be different, too.[1]

The architects of union sensed that "the product of their joint effort must be different." They realized that they were venturing into the unknown and that they were leaving many familiar land-

[1] *The Communion of Saints* (Toronto: United Church Publishing House, 1935), p. 15.

marks behind. At the inaugural service of The United Church of Canada in 1925, Dr. S. P. Rose recognized the break with tradition involved in union by preaching on the text, "Except a corn of wheat fall into the ground and die," and his theme must have been taken up by hundreds of preachers across the nation. The motto, "What hath God wrought," seriously considered by a committee appointed to design a seal for the United Church, suggests a similar conception of union as a new thing brought about by God.

Popular as it was with the promoters of union, however, the metaphor of the seed in the soil had surprisingly little effect upon its designers. The Basis of Union reveals no effort to adapt it to the needs of a twentieth-century church. E. L. Morrow and C. E. Silcox both complained in their studies of the church union movement that the doctrinal section of the Basis took almost no notice of contemporary trends in theology.[1] Silcox blamed the high average age of the committee members, observing also that biblical criticism was a very ticklish subject in Canada at the time. The same lack of boldness appears in other sections of the Basis. The framers apparently did not feel that it was part of their task to draft a polity or to suggest methods of ministerial settlement that would be appropriate for the peculiar needs of a Canadian church. Eschewing novelty, they undertook merely to construct out of existing materials a mutually acceptable statement.

If there is little in the Basis that seeks to anticipate the future, neither is there much evidence of an attempt to test the diverse traditions of the uniting churches by a return to origins. There was, indeed, ready recognition of a common heritage shared by Methodists, Presbyterians and Congregationalists. Dr. Pidgeon observed, with reference to arrangements for local co-operation, "the significant fact that not once, in all the negotiations that followed, was it ever suggested that any vital truth or principle was imperilled by leaving their people in charge of a minister of one of the negotiating churches."[2] The framers of the doctrinal section of the Basis of Union were able to compose fairly quickly a statement

[1]Silcox, *Church Union in Canada* (New York: Institute of Social and Religious Research, 1933), p. 137; Morrow, *Church Union in Canada* (Toronto: Allen, 1923), p. 129.

[2]*The United Church of Canada* (Toronto: Ryerson, 1950), p. 29.

embodying what they believed to be "a brief summary of our common faith." Those assigned the somewhat more arduous task of constructing polity could, without too much violence to the facts, conclude "that while the officers and courts of the negotiating churches may bear different names, there is . . . a substantial degree of similarity in the duties and functions of these officers and courts."

This sense of a substantial consensus is important as representing a major premise upon which the union was based, but it indicates no more than that the historic controversies that had divided the negotiating denominations were now widely regarded as dead issues. The record suggests that churches were not yet ready to grapple seriously with current sources of division. Otherwise it is difficult to account for the apparent readiness to accept as an insuperable barrier to negotiation the fact that Anglicans and Baptists had distinctive principles they were unwilling to surrender. The bitter division that took place among Presbyterians over the union had many causes, but the most important may well have been a lack of practice in dealing with even minor points of conscientious difference.

In any event, the union was brought about without any searching experience of bringing conflicting traditions before the bar of a common tradition. No one seems to have considered that in planning for a preliminary union it might be important to anticipate issues that would be raised in any project for a larger union. Some attention was indeed given to the problem of defining a valid ministry, but this was to satisfy the Church of Scotland and the whole discussion took for granted the familiar axioms of reformed theology. This failure to think in terms of the whole Christian tradition has encouraged the United Church to look inward. Despite rather perfunctory references in the Basis of Union to the authority of the ecumenical creeds, there has been a tendency to regard the formularies of the United Church as self-contained, and amateur ecclesiastical lawyers sometimes quote its *Manual* as if it had superseded twenty centuries of Christian practice.

The dominant note sounded by those who conceived a united church in Canada was neither the novelty of establishing a new tradition nor the authority commanded by a common tradition but the richness to be achieved by bringing diverse traditions together. Implicit in the enterprise, no doubt, was the thought that the denominational dowries represented parts of an original treasure that had been parcelled out and needed only to be brought together. The emphasis was on the diversity, however, and on the sharing that union would bring.

As early as 1874 George Monro Grant, later Principal of Queen's University, described his vision of unity to the Evangelical Alliance. His words deserve extensive quotation, for they set a pattern that was to be followed by unionist speakers over the years.

God will give us the church of the future. It shall arise in the midst of us, with no sound of hammer heard upon it, comprehensive of all the good and beauty that He has evolved in history. To this church, Episcopacy shall contribute her comely order, her faithful and loving conservatism; and Methodism impart her enthusiasm, her zeal for missions, and her ready adaptiveness to the necessities of the country; the Baptist shall give his full testimony to the sacred rights of the individual; the Congregationalist his to the freedom and independency of the congregation; and Presbyterianism shall come in her massive, well-knit strength, holding high the Word of God; and when, or even before, all this comes to pass, that is, when we have proved our Christian charity, as well as our faithfulness, proved it by deeds, not words, who shall say that our Roman Catholic brethren, also, shall not see eye to eye with us, and seal with their consent that true unity, the image of which they so fondly love? Why not? God can do greater things even than this. And who of us shall say, God forbid?[1]

This eclectic approach to unity commended itself for a number of reasons. One of the favourite words in the religious vocabulary of the period was "life," commonly contrasted with doctrine or organization. Advocates of union found it natural to dwell upon the benefits of sharing living experience rather than on the difficulties of harmonizing doctrine or of combining procedures. The peculiarities of the Canadian situation favoured the same emphasis. The need for united effort in missionary tasks called for a pooling of resources. The one touchy doctrinal problem involved in the union was most readily dealt with by recognizing the elements of truth embodied in both Calvinist and Arminian formulations.

Most of all, perhaps, controversy within the Presbyterian Church encouraged insistence upon the continuity of the United Church

[1] W. L. Grant and F. Hamilton, *George Monro Grant* (Edinburgh: Jack, 1905), p. 155.

with its predecessors. Through several embattled years before 1925 the great question at issue was whether the United Church or a non-concurrent body could claim to be the legitimate successor to the existing Presbyterian Church, and it was essential to the unionist argument that Presbyterians should be assured that their heritage would be maintained unimpaired. Hard-fought issues tend to attract more than their rightful share of attention, and it may well be that continuity with the past came temporarily to be overvalued.

Preoccupation with sharing inheritances, rather than mere conservatism, may account for the lack of creative thought in the Basis of Union. The architects of union did not recognize the problems of the twentieth century as items on their agenda. Their task was to put existing beliefs and polities at the service of the new church, ironing our minor inconsistencies and fitting acceptable names to familiar things. We may be fervently thankful today that they saw their task in such modest terms. If they had attempted to codify an up-to-the-minute theology, or if they had tried to envisage a polity for the imagined future, the United Church would be burdened with a constitution hopelessly out of date and a creed far more troublesome to consciences than the Athanasian ever was.

On June 10, 1925, when The United Church of Canada was constituted at a great inaugural service in the Mutual Street Arena in Toronto, the sharing of denominational heritages was the theme stressed in the official act of union. The elected leaders of the three churches spoke in turn of the manifestations of the Spirit most prominently associated with their traditions, each concluding with the statement, "Receive ye our inheritance among them that are sanctified." The same theme has been recalled at anniversaries ever since.

With this background of discussion, it was natural that one of the first concerns of the new church should be to assert its continuity with the uniting denominations. Delegations were quickly dispatched to Britain to secure from the parent churches their recognition of the new offspring. Membership was quickly claimed and granted in the International Congregational Council, the Oecumenical Methodist Conference and the World Alliance of Reformed Churches. United Church delegates have continued to participate actively in these organizations, although when in the denominational sessions at Amsterdam our representatives were assigned to a group of assorted united churches from the Orient there was some feeling that at last we had found our natural associates.

At home, members of The United Church of Canada began to test the mutual cross-fertilization of which so much was expected. They were not disappointed. Veterans of union days have often described the thrill of having their horizons lifted in unexpected ways by sharing worship and fellowship in unfamiliar forms and settings. They were prepared to feel the loss of much that was treasured, they said, but the new experience transcended in richness anything they had known. We have grown accustomed to the ease with which we draw upon a variety of traditions. Not many years ago, however, a visitor to Canada was amazed by an incident at the Berwick Camp Meeting in Nova Scotia. One of the features of this typically Methodist assembly was a hymn-sing devoted to requests from the congregation, and the visitor was astonished when four out of six requests were for the Twenty-third Psalm in metre set to as many different tunes.

Part of the richness of coming together was found in freedom from the uniting traditions. Denominationalism nourishes a sense of pious obligation to the memories of founders that makes for loyalty but can at times be oppressive. It was with some relief, therefore, that many United Churchmen found themselves unburdened of the rather formidable shadow of John Wesley or escaped from a ceaseless round of psalm tunes. Denominational mannerisms began to be discarded, and soon denominational memories began to fade. Although divisions remained, it was refreshing to be able to say "I am of Christ" rather than "I am of Apollos."

In this release from old limitations there was both promise and danger. United Churchmen felt a new freedom to experiment, and in a rapidly changing society this freedom imparted a mobility and flexibility that was often envied by other churches. The danger was that experiment might consist merely of adopting new gimmicks and peter out in faddishness. For a time the danger seemed to outweigh the promise. Concerned presbyters lamented that the United Church was "going Congregationalist," meaning that ministers and congregations were acting lawlessly in disregard of church courts. Outsiders whispered, "The United Church has no theology." The picture of anarchy was often grossly overdrawn, but there was a real peril that in escaping the bondage of partial traditions the United Church might throw tradition over altogether. No longer hampered by the inertia of inbred religious folkways, contemporary secular patterns threatened to take over.

One seldom hears any more the old gibes about formlessness and unpredictability. For better or worse The United Church of Canada has evolved a recognizable corporate image. A United Church young people's society or men's group is unlikely to be confused with its counterpart in any other denomination. When the musical review *Spring Thaw* set out to satirize the churches, the actor representing a United Church minister had no difficulty in getting his audience to recognize the caricature. More significantly, the United Church has long had a well-defined public stance on moral and social issues.[1] In worship too, despite variations in order, one can count fairly well on the general effect. On Sunday mornings an informal seemliness will prevail, with preaching dominant but prayer and praise seldom perfunctory. At Communion seasons the ritual may vary, but since the early years of union an almost universal method of distributing the elements has given a recognizable appearance to the service. Baptisms will take place, almost always now, during the morning service. On Sunday evenings the church will be nearly empty.

It could be argued that the United Church has become one of Canada's most homogeneous denominations. Congregations differ tremendously in background and outlook, but few can be assigned to definite categories like the high and low or the fundamentalist and liberal of other denominations. Party divisions within denominations are usually the result of ministerial initiative. Within the United Church there is little pressure upon a minister to conform as an individual, but it is exceptionally difficult for a minister to mould a congregation to his image. There is a fair measure of lay control, and initiative for change comes largely from a central bureaucracy. Except in large cities there is a rapid turnover of pastorates, so that individual enthusiasms cancel out over a period and the denominational pattern persists. Radical experimenters have their greatest

[1]There is, however, a curious divergence between national and local postures on such issues. Many laymen disregard the advice of board secretaries on matters of personal behaviour, but few of them suffer any embarrassment in their own congregations for doing so.

chance of success in inner city congregations supervised by the Board of Home Missions, but even in these a core of old-time members is usually able to prevent spectacular innovation.

No communion likes to think of itself as merely one denomination among many, but Christian history records many movements that set out to fertilize the life of the whole church, then settled down to cultivate their new truth in sectarian isolation. This could be the fate of the United Church unless the original vision of union is constantly renewed and pursued. There are many who welcome the appearance of the familiar signs of denominational identity. Never comfortable in a situation where some of the lines of definition were blurred, they have been only too happy to have a local habitation and a name like the rest. The eagerness with which congregations have adapted the United Church seal and crest to liturgical uses never intended for it is striking evidence of this nostalgia for denominational lares and penates. Such trends to conformism could have fatal consequences, for no tradition is more constricting than one that is still untempered by the centuries.

In one sense the United Church has certainly established a tradition of its own. Over the years it has succeeded in attracting the loyalty of its people and in giving them a sense of belonging together. In the early days of union, visitors occasionally remarked that they could see only a mixture of diverse elements. Congregations seemed as Methodist or Presbyterian as ever, and what sort of union was that? Even then the criticism was largely due to a misunderstanding, for few had learned to distinguish unity from uniformity and to recognize a common intent that made outward diversity irrelevant. Today it is almost never heard. The United Church of Canada began to take shape as a church from the moment of its inauguration, and the challenge of coping with a depression and churching suburbia has completed the process. Morale is so high, indeed, that outsiders sometimes complain that we act as if we were *the* church in Canada.

The results of church union have justified the hopes of those who many years ago urged a union of the churches. The essential values of the uniting traditions have been conserved and blended, and the result as anticipated has been mutual enrichment. Once in a while one hears complaints that one of the traditions, usually the Methodist, has been submerged by the others. Such complaints are infrequent, and derive their plausibility from a misconception of the actual state of Canadian Methodism—and Presbyterianism—in 1925. Doubtless some of the patina has rubbed off the denominational stones in the course of erecting the new structure. Doubtless some denominational enthusiasms have not taken fire in the new fellowship. No one could have expected otherwise. The founders did not anticipate that the United Church would feel like its predecessors.

Granted the success of the union in fulfilling the hopes of its promoters, however, the most important question pertaining to this study has yet to be asked. I have suggested that the framers of the Basis of Union did not find it necessary to do much delving into the sources of the church's faith and life. Have their successors compensated for the omission? As Wesley and Knox have taken their places in the perspective of church history, has there been a corresponding rediscovery of Chrysostom and Aquinas, of Cranmer and Menno Simons? Has there been a reawakening to the importance of what we are learning to call "the Christian tradition" as distinguished from the traditions of the various communions?

The answers to these questions must on the whole be disappointingly negative. The experience of belonging to a united church has not excited as much desire to examine the richness of the entire Christian heritage as one might have expected. From the first, indeed, The United Church of Canada has enthusiastically supported the ecumenical movement in all its phases and has shown itself ready to discuss terms of union or co-operation or mutual understanding with anyone. There has not been a corresponding eagerness to lay claim as of right to all things that are Christ's. For the most part the United Church has regarded itself as substantially the heir of its predecessors: Protestant, evangelical, puritan. In its practice it has borrowed most readily from churches of corresponding tradition in the United States. Theologically it has depended on Barth and Brunner, on Niebuhr and Tillich, and on the divines of the Church of Scotland. One reason for this apparent readiness to be satisfied with the gains of 1925 may be the presence in strength of the Anglican Church. Relations between United and Anglican churches are extremely friendly, but each tends to define its identity in relation to the other and therefore to emphasize points of difference. If the United Church thinks of itself primarily as the sum of its parts rather than as a microcosm of the Catholic Church, however, the main reason is that its founders so conceived it.

From the beginning, fortunately, there has been some recognition that a church committed to further union has both a right and a responsibility to lay claim to the whole Christian heritage. This recognition has been most explicit among those charged with devising forms of worship, and its outstanding monuments are *The Hymnary* and *The Book of Common Order*. Both of these the church owes largely to the vision of a few individuals. Even before union Dr. Alexander MacMillan had imparted his catholicity of taste to *The Book of Praise* prepared for the Presbyterian Church in Canada. In *The Hymnary*, of which he was editorial secretary, wide representation of "the Hymnody of the Church Universal" became the first principle of selection, taking precedence even over the aim of providing "a hymnody true to the genius, history, and tradition of the Communions which now compose The United Church of Canada."

In *The Book of Common Order*, prepared by Dr. H. Richard Davidson and Dr. Hugh Matheson, the same priority holds. According to the Preface, the aim of the committee was "to set forth orders that are loyal to the Spirit of Christ and loyal to the experience of the Church of all ages and of all lands; orders that carry on the devotional usage of the three uniting Communions in their living integrity." The book carries out the intention. Continuity with orders of the uniting churches is apparent, but the editors frequently corrected Reformed and Anglican idiosyncrasies by borrowing from Roman or eastern usage. For example, Sundays are measured not after Trinity but after Pentecost, and reference to early practice has led to a strengthening of the eucharistic thanksgiving. The committee now revising *The Book of Common Order*, unhampered by pressure to give equal weight to the customs of the uniting churches, is in touch with all aspects of the current wave of liturgical renewal.

Otherwise the most conspicuous sign of awareness of a common tradition is a subtle feeling of churchiness upon which many observers have commented. Church architecture and symbolism, although often betraying theological and liturgical amateurism, have indicated a desire to be in the main stream of the life of the church. Such a gesture as the inclusion of a Russian icon in the chapel of The United Church House, although trifling in itself, indicates a readiness to think of the United Church as more than a union of three Protestant denominations. Our failure to exploit more thoroughly the breadth of the Christian heritage is due to lack of initiative rather than to lack of openness.

The most conspicuous weakness of The United Church of Canada has been the lack of any serious effort to test its life and work by the touchstone of Christian tradition, whether in Scripture or in the experience of the church in other times and places. The result is that we have too often been contemporary and experimental without being venturesome or radical. Despite our willingness to learn from others, we have suffered from a strange lack of self-criticism. We tend to accept the validity of what we say and do because we have said and done it before. Perhaps our prosperity has been our undoing. There are, fortunately, refreshing signs of change. The New Curriculum now being prepared for our Sunday church schools is based upon a set of theological presuppositions that were wrestled over for many months. New programmes for laymen and lay-women reflect not merely the trend of the times but a theological rediscovery of the role of the laity in the church. Our Committee on the Christian Faith has made headlines simply by drawing upon elements of tradition not usually associated with us by the public.

As yet, however, we do not find in the Christian tradition the possibilities of radical renewal sensed by some of our European brothers of the Reformed tradition. In such experiments as the Iona Community and the French monastic brotherhood at Taizé they are seeking to make the timeless contemporary and to relate the present world to the eternal order. We have no counterparts yet, although there are stirrings among some of the younger men.

We should like to be catalysts of further reunion. Our fitness for that task will depend on our readiness to put our denominational life in the crucible of tradition. We have justified the belief of our fathers that traditions can be enriched by combination. The next step depends on our heeding their other word that a seed must die if it is to be the bearer of new life.

12

A CANADIAN CHRISTIAN TRADITION

H. H. WALSH

The purpose of this concluding chapter is to discover those elements
in Canadian development that have contributed to the formation of
a Canadian Christian tradition. It is obvious that in a country so
diversified, both politically and culturally, as Canada, this is a
formidable task; but the very variety of Canadian life has to a large
extent given Canada its own peculiar national development. Our
task, then, is to seek out, in the midst of conflicting interests, the
main determinants in Canadian history and to estimate their
contribution to a Canadian Christian tradition. There is also the
subdued hope that such a search may reveal a Canadian expression
of all that the Catholic Church stands for.

I

Canada has been described as "the child of political deadlock",[1] a
deadlock caused by cultural and religious antipathies that seemingly
had paralyzed the functioning of representative government.
Canada's birth can be regarded from a more positive point of view,
however, as a bold resolve on the part of "two warring nations" to
live together in peace and harmony on the basis of mutual toleration
of one another's peculiar ways of life. Admittedly, this resolve has
been "more honoured in the breach than the observance"; nevertheless, for almost a century two distinct cultures, going their own
separate ways, have continued to live together within one political
framework. There have been grave crises, but these have never been
allowed to reach the stage of civil war. According to a most diligent

[1]Goldwin Smith, quoted by Sir John Willison in *The Federation of Canada
1867-1917*, by several authors (Toronto, 1917), p. 41.

student of "Canadians in the making" this "is one of the minor miracles of history."[1] Such a miracle, we may be sure, would not have occurred unless these two cultures had something in common.

As a matter of fact they have much in common. First and foremost, there is a peculiarly Canadian outlook, which may be described in one word "loyalism."[2] The word is perhaps more applicable to English- than to French-speaking Canada, for it originated in the Thirteen Colonies and was imported into British North America by refugees from the American Revolution. Briefly, it came into being in opposition to the compact theory of government and "stood for the recognition of law as against rebellion in any form, for the unity of empire as against a separate independence of the colonies, and for monarchy instead of republicanism."[3] All this accorded well with French Canada's loyalty to the political and social ideals of seventeenth-century France.

Although the two loyalties have many differences in content, they have enough in common to induce both cultures to react in similar ways to the great social upheavals that were occurring during the eighteenth and nineteenth centuries in Europe and America. It was in the spirit of loyalism that English-speaking Canadians rejected the American Revolution and thus became distinguished from "Americans"; it was in the spirit of loyalism that French-speaking Canadians rejected the French Revolution and were saved from becoming modern Frenchmen.[4]

Perhaps even more significant in creating a basis for a common Canadianism was a third rejection, that of the Enlightenment. The closest either of the Canadas came to the Enlightenment, which has played such a prominent role in shaping reform movements in the rest of the new world,[5] was during the rebellious era of the 1830's. Two rebellions in 1837, one led by William Lyon Mackenzie, an admirer of the Scottish reformer Joseph Hume, the other by Louis Papineau, a devout student of Voltaire, were inspired by the

[1]A. R. M. Lower, *Canadians in the Making* (Toronto, 1958), p. 301.

[2]*Cf.* H. H. Walsh, *The Christian Church in Canada* (Toronto, 1956), pp. 102-115.

[3]A. G. Flick, *Loyalism in New York During the American Revolution* (New York, 1901), p. 16.

[4]*Cf.* Lower, *op. cit.*, pp. 121ff.

[5]*Cf.* J. T. Lanning, "The Enlightenment in Relation to the Church" in *History of Religion in the New World* (Conference Reports, Washington, D.C., 1958), pp. 153-160.

spirit of the Enlightenment as expounded by the philosophical radicals who achieved the great Reform Bill in the British Parliament of 1832.[1] The failure of these two rebellions meant that Canada was destined to follow the way of moderation, rather than to make any radical departure in political or social structure.

There was one movement of nineteenth-century Europe, replete with religious significance, that did not appear to be inimical to the spirit of loyalism, and that was accepted readily by both cultures in Canada—the Romantic Movement. Not only did this movement fit well into the framework of loyalism, but it also added, as it were, a divine afflatus to the Canadian's consciousness of the vast space in which he is called upon to build a nation.[2] The missionary societies and religious orders that arose out of the Romantic Movement in Europe were largely responsible for importing the new mood to Canada. The journeys of these missionaries in the northwest, faithfully recorded in religious journals, did much to excite a Canadian dream of a great nation from sea to sea.[3]

Such a prospect was enlarged upon by one of the fathers of Confederation, Georges-Etienne Cartier. In a speech urging the Canadian government to assume the administration of the Hudson's Bay Company's territories, he said, "our Canada [then] will extend as it did in the days when it was explored on all sides by our Fathers of the French race from the Atlantic to the Pacific. We will restore the national boundaries as the historical emergencies gradually are straightened out. From ocean to ocean a new life will reanimate all this part of North America."[4] It remained for another great Canadian romantic, George Monro Grant, to fill out Cartier's vision by affirming, "Thank God we have a country. It is not our poverty of land or sea that shall urge us to be traitors.[5]

There can be little question that the most dynamic aspect of the Canadian way of life is this feeling for space: space to roam in, space in which men of all nationalities, creeds and traditions may settle down alongside one another and do and believe as they please. It

[1]Cf. W. Kilbourn, *The Firebrand* (Toronto and Vancouver, 1956), pp. 86ff.
[2]Cf. Lower, *op. cit.*, pp. 358ff.
[3]Cf. Walsh, *op. cit.*, pp. 241-260, on missionary development in Canada.
[4]Quoted by Thomas Chapais, *Cours d'Histoire du Canada* (Quebec, 1934), Vol. VIII, p. 212.
[5]G. M. Grant, *Ocean to Ocean* (Toronto, 1877), p. 363.

was in such a mood that the great northwest was peopled by "'peculiar peoples' who sought in bloc settlements to preserve their religion and their ways of life."[1] Thus imperceptibly Canada changed from a bicultural to a multicultural nation in which variety rather than uniformity is encouraged. Indeed, variety has now become a way of life that stands in sharp contrast to modern nationalism with its emphasis upon homogeneity. Instead of saluting one flag and pledging allegiance to "one nation indivisible," Canadians salute many flags and hold tenaciously to various regional loyalties.

By no stretch of the imagination, then, can a Canadian identity be sharply etched; nevertheless, there has emerged on the North American continent a unique Canadian approach to national and international affairs. This approach became evident and has remained consistent ever since Canada emerged from a colonial status and assumed her place as a responsible self-governing nation within the community of nations.

Apart from the particular circumstances already alluded to, there remains to be considered a unique element in Canadian development that is more responsible than anything else for what is consistent in Canada's outlook: the existence of a French-Canadian nationalism. Whatever misgivings there may be about a Canadian identity, there need be none about a French-Canadian identity. It is this identity which has given the whole of Canada, including the Canadian church, ts peculiar development since the British Conquest in 1759, and it will continue to shape Canadianism unmistakably in the future.

Such an identity was evident almost from the first days of colonization. This early emergence of a peculiar people on the North American continent was possible because the original settlers in New France came mostly from one area in old France, Normandy and the adjacent territories, and because the cessation of immigration allowed a few thousand original settlers to people the colony by means of a high birth-rate.[2] As Father Grandpré has stressed in an earlier article in this book, the French-Canadians worked out one language before this had been done in France; there was one

[1]C. A. Dawson, *Group Settlement: Ethnic Communities in Western Canada* (Toronto, 1936), p. ix.

[2]*Cf.* Lower, *op. cit.*, for an interesting comment on "reproductive valour in New France," accompanied by a chart, pp. 33-34.

juridical system in New France, whereas in old France there were some three hundred. Thus from the beginning New France was a homogeneous state with a common language and a uniformity of outlook that was greatly dependent upon an indigenous catechism. All of this put it in sharp contrast to old France with its infinite variety of views.

In this new society the church took a role of leadership that was never granted to her in France itself. Although Gallicanism could not be completely excluded from the colony, it was never allowed to reach the heights of clerical defiance in Canada that it did in France; consequently, ultramontanism or loyalty to the papacy became a characteristic of French-Canadian life. This was possible because the kings of France were willing as an aid to colonization to allow French colonies closer contact with the Roman see than they would permit in France. Church authorities soon recognized that by deference to a pope far away they could secure greater freedom for the church at home.

Although the church was thus enabled to guide political and social development in New France to an extent hitherto unknown in France, it was compelled to make concessions to the new-world environment. The ease with which a settler could move away from church control into the vast spaces of North America fostered a democratic spirit that did not fail to have its influence upon church polity. As Father Grandpré emphasizes,[1] not the seigneur but the captain of militia, an *habitant* elected by his peers, and the church wardens, elected by parishioners, became responsible along with the curé for the material aspects of local religious life.[2]

This concession to frontier democracy was closely linked with an immediate supervision by priest and bishop of every aspect of communal life; consequently, when the British took possession of the colony they found it impossible to rule their new subjects except through the mediation of parochial authorities. As she was facing serious disaffection among her Thirteen Colonies to the south, Britain was inclined to welcome this method of rule as the surest way of securing the loyalty of the French-Canadians. Also, to

[1]*Supra*, p. 3.
[2]*Cf*. M. Roy, *The Parish and Democracy in French Canada* (Toronto, 1950), p. 17ff.

secure greater loyalty from church authorities she allowed the church to continue to tithe the people and permitted French Canada to retain the civil law and feudal practices of the old regime. Thus there grew up, in the heart of Canada, an ecclesiastical society based upon a close alliance between priest and people.

II

Such a solid and impregnable phalanx of Roman Catholicism could not fail to have a profound influence upon the development of Protestantism in Canada. In the first place, the British government hoped that its concession to the Roman Catholic Church was only a temporary measure and was anxious to set up a strongly established Protestant Church that might in time replace the former even in French Canada. It hoped that the Church of England would serve this purpose. Failing this, it was ready to accept a combination of Anglican and Presbyterian church establishments,[1] and even to associate the Roman Catholic Church in such an arrangement.

The variety of racial stocks and religious allegiances of the immigrants who followed the conquest soon made this a vain hope. Even if conditions for the creation of an established church had been more propitious than they turned out to be, none of the traditional churches of Europe or America would have been equal to the challenge presented by frontier life in the closing days of the eighteenth century. The obvious task before the churches was the reorganization of the social life of an uprooted people, many of whom had abandoned established *mores* and had developed intemperate habits.

Most of the contributors to this symposium have remarked upon the weakness of the established churches of Europe and America during the early settlement of British North America, particularly their lack of enthusiasm for missionary work and their ineptitude in dealing with colonial peoples. The Anglican clergy for the most part took as their textbook on morals and manners *The Whole Duty of Man*, which proclaimed "that rigid class divisions were divinely

[1] *Cf.* A. B. Warburton, *A History of Prince Edward Island* (Saint John, N.B., 1923), p. 390, for an example of a double establishment that was attempted for a time.

ordained, and that all good subjects must faithfully perform their duties in those particular situations of life wherein it has pleased God to place them.[1] Unfortunately these were the morals and manners that the first Anglican bishops in Canada, Charles Inglis in Nova Scotia and Jacob Mountain in Quebec, tried unsuccessfully to inculcate, with disastrous consequences for the future of the Church of England in Canada.

Nor did the Scottish Presbyterians have a more inspiring or comprehensive doctrine for the frontier. At the time that Canada was opened up to Scottish immigration, the Established Church of Scotland had come under the influence of the Enlightenment and was inclined to deprecate religious enthusiasm. Such an era of moderation did not produce missionary zeal or the spirit of self-sacrifice, so very few ministers of the Kirk volunteered to go to Canada.[2]

It is the same story when we turn to nonconformity. "For the nonconformists," says a recent student of the era, "the eighteenth century was a placid and unheroic age. Their forefathers had arisen in their wrath to bring down king and bishops, but scarcely an echo of the old zeal survived."[3] Nonconformity in Canada was represented by New England Congregationalists who arrived in fairly large numbers in Nova Scotia in the middle of the eighteenth century. Congregationalism (or Independency, as it was known in England) had in New England assumed the unusual role of an established church; but when it might have taken over the organization of the social life of Nova Scotia it was at a peculiarly low ebb in its homeland. For this reason it never became a major denomination in Canada.

As a result of the failure of the traditional churches of Great Britain and America to provide for the religious need of the frontier there was a decided weakening of religious interest in British North America and a definite need for a drastic religious awakening; the

[1]*Cf.* J. W. Bready, *England: before and after Wesley* (London, 1938), p. 85.

[2]*Cf.* G. Patterson, *Memoir of the Rev. James MacGregor, D.D.* (Philadelphia, 1859), p. 220; also J. H. S. Burleigh, *A Church History of Scotland* (Oxford, 1960), p. 29ff.

[3]G. R. Cragg, *The Church and the Age of Reason* (Harmondsworth, 1960), p. 132.

awakening when it came was in part an angry revolt against the traditional churches and resulted in the formation of new religious groupings.[1]

III

Thus arose the sectarian tradition in Canada which, as Professor Moir points out,[2] waxes in periods of frontier expansion and wanes in periods of prosperous consolidation. It has remained a constant element in Canadian social development because the frontier has never been closed. Immigration and the frequent occurrence of depressions in some of the long-established areas of Canada, such as the Maritimes, continue to feed the flame of sectarian revolt against conventional churches.

One of the peculiar traits of sectarianism in Canada has been its initiative in the formation of political parties.[3] At first sight this seems to be a strange activity for other-worldly religions, but as Barbara Ward has emphasized in her study *The Rich Nations and the Poor Nations*,[4] the eschatological idea so prominent in any sect movement can easily be transmuted into this-worldly terms. Such a transmutation, which seems to occur among pre-millennial sects more readily in Canada than in other countries, has hastened the evolution of sects into churches.

A transformation quickly took place within the Baptist community in the Maritimes. The Baptist Church had become the heir of a Newlight revolt against Congregationalism in Nova Scotia, but when it accepted political responsibility in the field of educational and social reform it soon moved from a sect to a church type of religion. Later it became subject to the same type of sectarian revolt as the Anglicans, Presbyterians and Congregationalists had experienced at an earlier period. Because of this constant sectarian upheaval within their community, the Baptists have never been able to achieve a genuine national church structure in Canada.

Other denominations have faced similar problems. The Lutheran

[1]*Cf.* S. D. Clark, *Church and Sect in Canada* (Toronto, 1948), esp. p. xi, for comment on this phenomenon.

[2]*Supra*, p. 121.

[3]*Cf.* Walsh, *op. cit.*, pp. 308ff.

[4]*Cf.* B. Ward, *The Rich Nations and the Poor Nations* (New York, 1962), pp. 22ff.

Church, for example, has failed as yet to complete a national structure despite a continuous history in Canada since 1772. This failure is due partly to the language barrier among various ethnic groups but partly also to the fact that recent Lutheran immigrants to Canada are displaced and uprooted people who are peculiarly open to the appeal of enthusiastic sects.[1]

Churches closely allied to Eastern Orthodoxy are also subject to sectarian inroads. Their strength comes in the first place as conservators of old-country ethnic customs and historic prejudices. Such a function, however, seems to breed discontent in the new world; and just as in an earlier day Anglican and Scottish churches attempting to be conservators of British ideals were angrily attacked by Newlight sects, so today new sects are causing severe embarrassment to Orthodoxy and its allies.[2]

Apparently this must continue to be a normal procedure in Canadian religious development. As long as Canada continues to receive, without adequate preparation for settlement, large numbers of immigrants, these will continue to repeat a familiar cycle: a period of disorganization and a search for a new orientation, which is generally found within the "community of saints" of some enthusiastic sect. During this period there will be confusion of outlook among the churches to which these immigrants belong as well as among the sects to which they may turn in their search for a new social status. All of this is part of Canada in the making; what these new peoples will contribute to a future Canadianism or to the Christian church in Canada must necessarily remain in the realm of speculation.

IV

Some tentative idea of the road these sects and the churches they now menace may follow can be gleaned from a study of the sects and churches that have passed through this disturbed phase of their development and have now reached a mature adjustment to new-world conditions. The church that best illustrates the transition from sectarianism to a new-world church type of religion is the

[1] *Cf.* W. E. Mann, *Sect, Cult and Church in Alberta* (Toronto, 1955), p. 33.
[2] *Ibid.*, p. 56.

Methodist, now embraced in The United Church of Canada. Methodism has long been recognized by Canadian historians as one of the determining influences in shaping the national character of English-speaking Canada, as well as the ecclesiastical outlook of many of the older churches. One reason for this, and perhaps the most significant, is that Methodism was an early projection of the Romantic Movement which found an enthusiastic reception on the Canadian frontier. In time, the older churches were also stimulated and revitalized by this movement, but Methodism under the guidance of John Wesley had developed in the eighteenth century a warm evangelical approach to disinherited people that allowed it to compete on even terms with the Newlight sects on the western frontiers of both the United States and Canada.

Methodism first came to central Canada by way of the United States, where it had already been affected by the frontier. Its activism rather than pietism became a characteristic of Canadian as well as American Christianity, for the other churches found that if they were to hold their own on the open frontier they had to follow the Methodist example. They did so in many other matters as well; an itinerant ministry, voluntary support of the clergy by congregations, as few doctrinal tests as possible, were parts of the Methodist equipment that all the other churches were to adopt in one way or another.

Many of these things were at first greatly resented by the more conventional churches; even the conservative Wesleyan Methodist ministers who began to replace American Methodist missionaries after the outbreak of war with the United States in 1812 were critical of many of these frontier techniques and produced some bitter schisms within Methodism; but with the rise of evangelical fervour within all the older churches much of the acerbity in religious rivalry began to disappear. This was particularly so in the great northwest, where missionary societies and religious orders rooted in the Romantic Movement began to co-operate with the Canadian government in opening up this area to human habitation.

On this new frontier the Methodists again pioneered when the Wesleyan Missionary Society sent into the Hudson's Bay Company's territory James Evans, one of the great romantic figures of missionary enterprise.[1] The Anglicans also had their very romantic Bishop Bompas, the founder of three dioceses in the furthest northwest. Nor did the Roman Catholics lag behind in this new mood, for a very romantic religious order, The Oblates of Mary, produced the adventurous Father Lacombe, the peacemaker among the Crees and Blackfoot. All of these missionaries came from Europe, but they stimulated the Canadian churches to undertake vast missionary enterprises in the northwest and this prepared them to play a prominent role in opening up that part of the country to settlement and industrial exploitation.

During the period of western expansion the churches produced some remarkable missionary statesmen. The Roman Catholic Archbishop Taché and the Anglican Archbishop Machray both played prominent roles in the creation of the province of Manitoba. Most energetic of all was James Robertson, the Presbyterian superintendent of missions, whose tremendous missionary projects in the west created to some extent the circumstances that made a united church of Canada almost an inevitable outcome.[2]

These men and their colleagues in the missionary field were in a profound sense the begetters of a greater Canada (from sea to sea). They have bequeathed to former sectarian and conventional churches alike a tradition of close affinity of politics and religion coupled with a deep sense of responsibility for national welfare.

V

This concern for national welfare helped to bring about Confederation; and when Confederation became a fact, the churches were immediately challenged to make their ecclesiastical structures conterminous with the new national state. This process strengthened even further the tradition of political responsibility and also added another dimension to the Canadian Christian tradition: a search for unity.

The creation of territorial churches necessitated a long series of church unions, until church union negotiations became almost a permanent feature of Canadian church life. When the consolidations

[1]*Cf.* J. H. Riddell, *Methodism in the Middle West* (Toronto, 1946), p. 22.
[2]*Cf.* Walsh, *op. cit.*, p. 288ff.

were completed it was seen that the largest territorial church in Canada was the formerly much-divided Methodist, with a membership at the time of the census of 1891 of 861,666, being 17.8 per cent of the population. The Presbyterians came next with a population of 770,119, or 15.1 per cent, followed by the Anglicans with a membership of 661,608 or 13.7 per cent. According to the same census the Roman Catholics numbered 2,009,201, or 41.6 per cent of the Canadian people. These four major denominations together constituted 90 per cent of the Canadian population, leaving 10 per cent divided among Lutherans, Baptists, Orthodox, Jews, Congregationalists and numerous sects.[1]

Thus within a quarter of a century after Confederation Canada had a predominantly church type of religious affiliation. The numerical strength of the various denominations has remained fairly constant down to the present time, with some significant variations. Roman Catholics now represent 45.7 per cent of the population, a significant gain; Anglicans retain about the same proportion as in 1891; Methodists, Congregationalists and a large proportion of Presbyterians, now embraced in The United Church of Canada, represent 20.1 per cent of the population, while the remaining Presbyterians retain 4.5 per cent of all Canadians.[2] These four major congregations now represent some 84 per cent of Canada's population, leaving 16 per cent to be apportioned to Lutheran, Orthodox, Baptist and Jewish communions. Since the Lutheran and Orthodox are fast-growing churches, it would appear that the sectarian groups are a diminishing influence in Canadian national life; nevertheless, the fastest-growing denomination in Canada is the Pentecostal Church,[3] reflecting, no doubt, the appeal of this warmly evangelical religion to the immigrants arriving in Canada during the last decade.

The most significant development during the era under consideration was the emergence of The United Church of Canada. Much emphasis has been placed upon the fact that the negotiation for this union began in western Canada, and there is little doubt that

[1]*Ninth Census of Canada 1951* (Ottawa, 1953), Vol. I, Table 37, contains "numerical and percentage distribution of the population by religious denominations" from 1871 to 1915.

[2]Press release by the Dominion Bureau of Statistics.

[3]*Ibid.*

western impatience forced the issue. This was due to the difficulty that all the major churches were experiencing in trying to provide adequate services to a population stretched out thinly along two transcontinental railways. Their failure in this matter had been a serious embarrassment to the churches, for the Canadian government was relying heavily upon them to provide moral and cultural guidance to new Canadians who were being transported in great numbers to the prairie provinces, and to shepherd and educate the aboriginal population.[1] These two responsibilities had for some time been a most pressing concern of home mission boards, and when these faltered, the scattered settlements began to create community churches adequate to their needs. As these appeared to serve the needs of the community far better than denominational churches, their members were fired with the idea that these churches should lead the way to nothing less than a national church of Canada.

VI

A national church of Canada was not just a western dream. It represents a deep-felt urge in Canadian life and a strong conviction in almost every major denomination. Particularly is this true of the Roman Catholic Church, which for a century and a half had been an established church in New France and still holds a semi-established position in the province of Quebec. The Anglican Church at the time of the Conquest had aspired to displace the Roman Catholic and to take over from it the responsibility of creating a homogeneous society in British North America. The Scottish Kirk was not adverse to such a project, but it wanted to share in the new establishment since it also was an established church within the British Empire. Among the Wesleyan Methodists there was some support for an Anglican establishment, with which they could co-operate as they did in England.

An upsurge of sectarianism in the early days of settlement made all attempts at an establishment futile; nevertheless, the ideal of a national church never quite faded from the Canadian consciousness but has continued to colour the outlook of the Canadian churches down to the present time. In this respect Canadian Christianity

[1]*Cf.* Walsh, *op. cit.*, p. 265ff.

stands in sharp contrast to American Christianity, which takes denominationalism as normal, so much so that one American church historian has boldly proclaimed that denominationalism is the "destiny which awaits the whole of the Catholic Church of the future."[1] The long series of church unions that are so prominent in Canadian church history, culminating in the formation of The United Church of Canada in 1925, is the historical expression of an ideal that looks beyond denominationalism as the final destiny of the church in Canada.

After Confederation the urge for church unity became particularly strong. The new Canadian nation was artificial, its unity a tender plant that required constant cultivation. Patriots soon recognized that religious controversy was a luxury in which they could indulge only at the peril of national disintegration. Successive crises provoked by conflicting cultural issues have compelled both Canadian statesmen and churchmen to exercise infinite patience in the search for solutions. It was by the exercise of infinite patience that Canadian statesmen brought Confederation about. It was by the exercise of infinite patience in negotiation that church leaders broke down sectarian and regional barriers to form territorial churches. And it was the experience gained in these earlier negotiations that made it possible to outflank even venerable church polities and bring into being The United Church of Canada.

VII

Some of the hopes aroused by this very great ecumenical victory have been disappointed. There are murmurs that the United Church has lost its original purpose to serve as a nucleus for a national church of Canada and has now become another denomination among many. No longer does it seem to aim at becoming that great church of the future as foretold by George Monro Grant in 1874: a church that embraces Anglican episcopacy, Methodist enthusiasm, Presbyterian scholarship and Congregational independency, and by its charity has the seal of Roman Catholic approval.[2] As has been

[1]L. J. Trinterud, "The Task of the American Church Historian," *Church History*, XXV (March, 1956), p. 9.
[2]*Supra*, p. 137.

suggested by one of our contributors, its failure to move forward along these lines may be due to its over-sensitive loyalty to its constituent traditions. In point of fact, nearly all our contributors have shown that the particular churches that they represent began in Canada as conservators of an old country tradition; so it is not surprising that those who negotiated for a united church of Canada endeavoured to remain loyal to this pioneer concern. Such a concern kept at least one-third of the Presbyterians outside the union, and no doubt many other Canadian denominations from participating in the negotiations.

This purely denominational concern was also buttressed by the Canadian national tradition of encouraging multi-cultural development. Consequently, there has been a noticeable absence in Canadian theological circles of any deep-seated concern for a maintenance of identity and continuity with a constitutive tradition such as has given birth to creative reform movements in Great Britain and on the continent of Europe. Movements like the Evangelical, the Oxford and neo-Orthodox have had their repercussions in Canada, but Canadian theologians for the most part have depended upon European theologians to bring about through fresh discovery and application a renewal of the Christian tradition. It is easy to understand, then, why there were no far-reaching revisions of the churches' formularies in the Basis of Union of The United Church of Canada nor any serious attempt on the part of the negotiators to set forth a creative tradition behind the traditions that had come together to form a *Koinonia* in which Christ would be more adequately manifested in Canadian national life.

It would be ironic indeed if The United Church of Canada, by its loyalty to those traditions which came together to form a great new church of the future, should perpetuate the same sort of conservatism that kept the Anglicans, Baptists and a sizable proportion of the Presbyterians out of the union of 1925—especially since this loyalty is in many cases to old-country traditions that have little relevance to Canadian conditions. Unfortunately the United Church did not in its formative days gain the sympathetic approval of the Roman Catholic Church, and this has prevented it from examining "the richness of the entire Christian heritage."[1] This may

[1]*Supra*, p. 142.

have been due to the fact that the need for a united Protestant church of Canada was too often put forward as necessary in the face of an aggressive Roman Catholic Church. Nor was the Roman Catholic Church without blame. As has been pointed out, the original impetus behind church union was the challenge of the west. When the major Protestant denominations tried to meet this challenge by united action, the uncharitable comment of the rector of the Roman Catholic Cathedral of Regina was, "This movement of Church-Union [indicated] the complete disintegration of Protestantism and the open condemnation of its fundamental principles."[1]

Happily such voices as these from out of the old quarrelsome days of denominational rivalry on the western frontier are very infrequently heard today. At the present time there is among the major churches of Canada the most friendly co-operation in all aspects of ecclesiastical life: in social welfare, in Christian journalism, in the formation of church societies for historical, theological and biblical research. It is also evident from the papers contributed to this symposium that the national purpose of Canada has imposed a somewhat similar polity upon all the churches; if the day ever comes for these churches to merge their ecclesiastical structures into one great new church, there will be little noticeable change in polity at the functional level at least.

Nor does it seem as improbable today as it was in 1925 that the Roman Catholic Church will be completely absent from the negotiations for such a reunion of Christendom in Canada. The Roman Catholic Church itself has initiated a "dialogue" with Protestant and Orthodox theologians. Those taking part in the dialogue are discussing with absolute frankness doctrinal differences and how these may be overcome.

The most hopeful aspect of this dialogue is that it may encourage the participants to transcend their multiple forms of interpretation by a renewed determination to find the constitutive tradition that has through all the centuries of separation made it possible for us, even at this late date, to recognize one another as, in some sense, members of the Body of Christ.

[1]G. T. Daly, *Catholic Problems in Western Canada* (Toronto, 1921), p. 114.

As a result of this new-found fellowship with their French-Canadian compatriots, many English-speaking Protestants, particularly in the province of Quebec, are now inclined to agree with George Monro Grant "that there is . . . in the very centre of our country, a Christian civilization that is not of our type, but that it is altogether beautiful from some points of view."[1] Nor would they any longer dismiss lightly as a vain hope that "the Head of the Church will find a way of uniting two great historic confessions of Christianity, that have so long stood face to face as enemies, in a church of the future greater than any existing church."[2]

[1] Quoted by John Oxley in *Men of the Day: A Canadian Portrait Gallery*, ed. by L. H. Taché (Montreal, 1894), p. 137.
[2] *Ibid.*